MAKING
MOSAICS

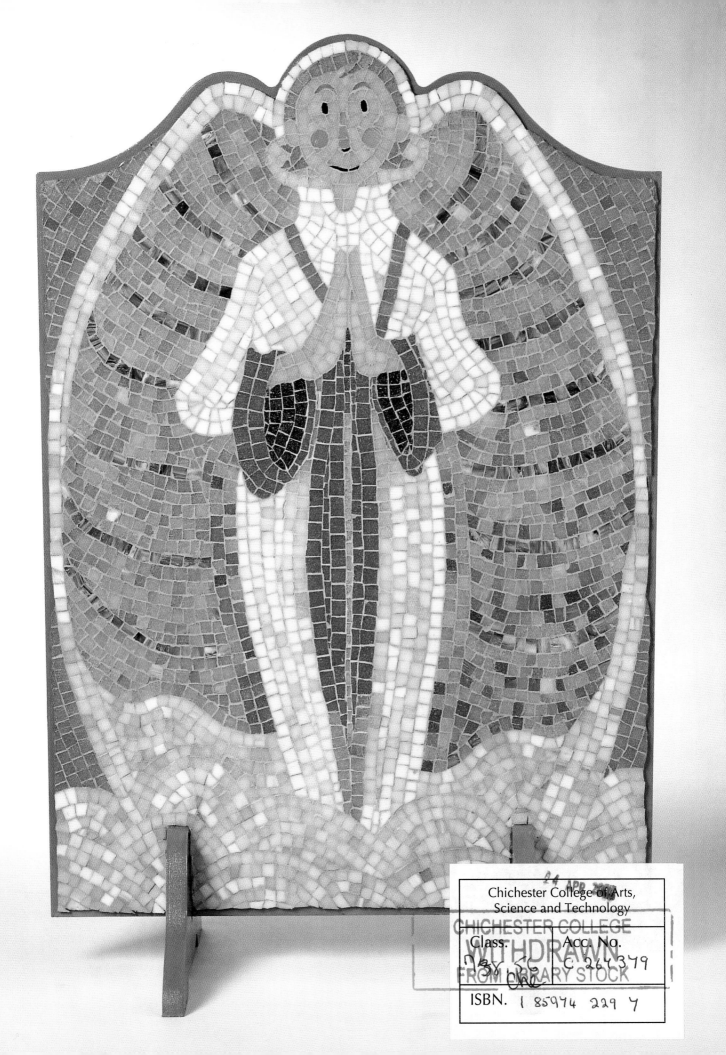

MAKING MOSAICS

MARTIN CHEEK

NEW HOLLAND

Published in 2000 by
New Holland Publishers (UK) Ltd
London • Cape Town
Sydney • Auckland

24 Nutford Place
London W1H 6DQ
United Kingdom

80 McKenzie Street
Cape Town 8001
South Africa

Level 1, Unit 4, 14 Aquatic Drive
Frenchs Forest, NSW 2086
Australia

Unit 1A, 218 Lake Road
Northcote, Auckland
New Zealand

ISBN 1 85974 229 7

Designer: Grahame Dudley
Photographer: Colin Bowling
Editor: Tessa Clark
Assistant Editor: Anke Ueberg

Editorial Direction: Rosemary Wilkinson

10 9 8 7 6 5 4 3 2 1

Reproduction by
PICA Colour Separation, Singapore
Printed and bound in Malaysia by
Times Offset (M) Sdn. Bhd.

Page 1: Russian Doll by Jo Letchford

Page 2: Angel Firescreen by Martin Cheek
(see pages 84-89)

This page: Indian Parrot by Martin Cheek

Facing page: Fiery Phoenix by Martin Cheek
(see also page 89)

Dedication

This book is dedicated to the artists

of the future – long may they continue to

look to the past. (This obsession with

everything always having to be "new"

should be constantly challenged.)

Contents

Introduction

When my first step-by-step book of mosaics, *Mosaics in a Weekend*, came out in 1997, mosaic was undergoing something of a renaissance. The media, magazines and the general public had realized that it was possible to make your own mosaics and that this "ancient art" was also very much a living contemporary craft. As if to prove this point, my second book, *Design Sourcebook: Mosaics*, containing 200 mosaics by 46 artists, became the first ever directory of contemporary mosaic. The public could now commission the artists directly or indeed become inspired enough to make mosaics for themselves.

In the meantime, I have for the past five years been holding monthly mosaic courses from our beautiful 18th-century home in Broadstairs, Kent. Over this period, more than 700 people have attended the courses, many going on to become professional mosaic artists in their own right, whilst others have taken up mosaic as a hobby and continue to make beautiful mosaics. (One of the many perks of my job is to receive the latest pictures of these.) I am also proud of the fact that, as a result of the courses, many people have now visited the beautiful seaside town of Broadstairs who might otherwise not have done so.

About the projects

The projects in this book have been designed very much with accessibility in mind. There are templates for all the relevant projects and these can be enlarged on a photocopier. MDF blanks are available direct from the suppliers. Adhesives, grout, tools and safety equipment are widely available from DIY outlets.

Despite the popularity of mosaic as a pastime, it can still prove difficult to obtain mosaic tiles in small quantities, particularly if you need a wide variety of colours. In order to make getting started easier, mosaic tile packs are available from "Martin Cheek Mosaic Kits" for most of the projects in this book and also for those in the first book, *Mosaics in a Weekend* (also published by New Holland). Details of suppliers can be found at the back of this book.

I am continually amazed by the range of diverse styles that are possible, using what can seem to be such an inflexible material. I was delighted that four other professional mosaicists were willing to contribute to this book as well as my own team of assistants.

It was important to show styles other than my own which, try as I might, I am unable to do alone – my style is my style and I am stuck with it!

In designing the projects, we have tried to illustrate the wide range of styles, materials and techniques available to the modern mosaicist. There are projects for internal and external use, featuring direct and indirect mosaics. I doubt if the same people who are drawn to the Crazy Concrete Planter on page 38 would be similarly attracted to the painstaking process of mosaicing the Indian Elephant Tea Tray on page 66 or the Angel Firescreen on page 84 – it's "horses for courses", as the saying goes. Whichever projects you decide to tackle, I hope you derive as much fun and satisfaction from it as we did in putting this book together for you. Happy nibbling!

Martin Cheek

Heron #1. Martin Cheek

making mosaics/introduction

Getting Started

BASIC TOOLS

Mosaic Tile Nippers

Mosaic tiles are cut to shape using a special tool. These mosaic nippers, compared with, say, a pair of scissors, have an extremely high pivot point. The handles curve in towards the bottom and this is where you are meant to hold them. This gives the nippers maximum leverage, so you don't have to work so hard when you cut the tiles. The jaws of the nippers are made of tungsten carbide for strength and don't quite meet up when you close them – this is correct.

In contrast to a pair of scissors, nippers cut at right angles to the handles. One side juts out – this is the side used to cut the tiles in straight lines. Practise using the jaws the "wrong" way round and you will soon learn how to cut curved lines.

Tweezers and Cocktail Sticks

Sometimes it may be helpful to use a pair of tweezers or a cocktail stick to make fine adjustments to the position of tesserae.

Builder's Float

A builder's float is a square piece of wood about 30 x 30 cm (12 x 12 in). It has a handle on one side and is used to smooth or flatten sand, cement or concrete.

Glues

PVA (Polyvinyl Acetate) is the standard glue used for gluing the tesserae down when making a direct mosaic (see page 12). Although you can buy "waterproof" PVA, it is not recommended to put a direct mosaic made using PVA outdoors. In winter, moisture can seep in through the grout and freeze; as it freezes, it expands and forces the tesserae off the board.

PVA is perfect for indoor use, though: it does not smell and washes off easily with soap and water. When wet it is white, but as it sets it turns clear and forms a strong bond.

Wallpaper Paste and Water-Soluble Glue

The basic principle of indirect mosaic is to glue the tesserae temporarily to kraft paper, cement it to your rendered surface, then soak the paper off with warm water (see page 12). Thus the glue required needs to be water-soluble. I find wallpaper paste ideal for this. It's cheap, it lasts a long time and you can mix it to the consistency that you like. When working indirect, I prefer the glue to be fairly stiff. Children's paper paste in little pots with a rubber nozzle dispenser is also fine. Basically, any water-soluble glue will do the job.

Epoxy Resin

For outdoor purposes and when a stronger glue is required, epoxy resin is the answer. It is available from hardware and department stores and comes in tube or syringe form. I recommend the syringe type, as this ensures equal dispensing of the two parts. Mix the two parts together thoroughly with a metal modelling tool or lollipop stick. A metal modelling tool is stronger and more controllable; clean it with a scalpel once the glue has hardened. Quick-setting epoxy resin has a "working time" of about five minutes and a "setting time" of about 15 minutes. Slow-setting epoxy resin has a "working time" of about an hour and a "setting time" of about 16 hours.

Tile Adhesive

Ready-mixed adhesive is ideal, but slightly more expensive and with a shorter shelf life than the powdered variety. Most brands have to be "slump free", i.e. the mix should cling to the trowel without falling off. Follow the manufacturer's instructions.

MOSAIC MATERIALS

Vitreous Glass

"Vitreous" simply means non-porous. This material is used to clad swimming pools. The standard range consists of 50 colours and from time to time extra colours become available (snap these up whenever you see them). Since the majority of the market is for swimming pools, there is a better choice of blues, greens and whites than of other colours.

Vitreous glass tiles come in sheets of 15 x 15 tiles, each square measuring 2 x 2 cm (¾ x ¾ in). Each colour has a "series number", rather like oil paints. Very pale colours are the cheapest (series 1) and the brightest colours with metallic "veining" are the most expensive (series 4). For chemical reasons, "Candy Pink" makes it to series 5 all on its own.

The backing paper is soaked off by placing the sheet of tiles in a basin of hot water. After a few minutes the paper will float off. Remove it, rinse the tiles in more hot water and transfer them to a colander to drain, then spread them out onto a dry towel. Each colour can then be given its own jar.

Alternatively, vitreous glass tiles can be bought in large 25 kg boxes, sold as mixed "scrap" for about one third of the price of the tiled sheets. There is nothing wrong with these tiles – simply sort them by colour into their different containers. You can top up any extra colours you require by ordering them separately. It's a good idea to always have a mixed box available as it often contain colours which are not widely available or are from a different "batch" than the one you have bought, with a slightly different hue.

Ceramic

"Cinca" is the brand name of a type of unglazed ceramic tile made in Portugal (see Suppliers on page 94). It comes in sheets of 14 x 14 tiles, each square measuring 23 x 23 mm (1 x 1 in). Because it is heavier than vitreous, the glue binding it to the backing paper is stronger and therefore takes longer to soak off. Even then, the tiles tend to stick together whilst drying, so spread them out individually on the towel.

There are usually 25 different colours to choose from. Unlike vitreous glass tiles, either side of Cinca tiles can be used. The main difference between vitreous and Cinca is that vitreous glass is shiny and reflective, whereas Cinca is an unglazed, non-reflective ceramic. When placing an area of one next to the other, the vitreous will appear to come forward whilst the Cinca will appear to recede (see the Flower Hot Plate on page 50).

A mosaic made entirely of Cinca will have a calm effect, reminiscent of Indian art (see the Guinea Fowl Plaque on page 54). Cinca is excellent for floor mosaics as the tiles are completely flat.

Smalti

"Smalti" is the Roman word for "melt". Smalti is hand-made in Venice and until recently there were only three families still making it. The recipes and techniques have been kept secret and handed down through the generations. Glass is melted in a cauldron, then poured out onto a metal sheet where it is pressed down like a pizza which is then sawn up into little briquettes about 2 x 1 cm (¾ x ½ in). It is supposed to be used with the sides uppermost, thus emphasizing its rippled surface. Tiny air bubbles in smalti are part of its intrinsic quality.

Smalti can be bought as a 20 kg irregular mix box, known as "roti". This will contain tesserae that have a curved edge – these are the edges of the "pizza". Purists would argue that these shouldn't be used, but I find them invaluable for details.

Hand-made smalti is very expensive, but it makes a lovely addition to any mosaic and can be incorporated in small quantities.

Because of its uneven surface you do not need to grout smalti when working direct (see page 12). It "self grouts" – as you push the smalti into the tile adhesive, it is forced up between the gaps in the smalti.

Broken Crockery

This, too, is a wonderful material for mosaic. Some mosaic artists have made this medium their own. I don't find it as simple as it looks. To create a successful piece requires a good sense of colour and an eye for basic design.

Clockwise from top left: Jars of vitreous glass (note the ribbed undersides); sheets of vitreous in their "pre-soaked" state can be conveniently stacked in boxes; even a 25 kg box of vitreous mix can look attractive stored in a brightly coloured plastic box; Cinca ceramic tiles (note how flat they are); a 2 kg bag of smalti.

BASIC TECHNIQUES

To Cut a Tile into Four Square Tesserae

A vitreous glass tile measures 2 x 2 cm (¾ x ¾ in), so it is possible to cut one tile into four "tesserae", each of which will average 1 x 1 cm (⅜ x ⅜ in). (A "tessera" is the term used for any fragment of mosaic.) I say "average" because you will find that it is impossible to cut all of the tesserae into perfect squares. Don't worry about this, the slightly different shapes will give your mosaics the quality that you are looking for.

I suggest that you treat the 1 x 1 cm (⅜ x ⅜ in) tesserae as your "basic unit" from which to work. You will see that sometimes these units are "nibbled" into triangles or circles, but, as a bench mark, the 1 x 1 cm (⅜ x ⅜ in) dimension is a good one – any smaller and the work tends to become too fiddly. Using these dimensions, a square metre of mosaic will contain about 10,000 tesserae, i.e. just over 1000 tesserae per square foot.

To cut a tile into four pieces, hold the tile between your thumb and fingers with your thumb running down the left hand side of the tile as shown below. The nippers don't have to go too far into the tile – only about 3 mm (⅛ in). Gently squeeze the handles together and the tile will crack into two rectangles. Pick up a rectangle and make a bridge with it across your index and middle finger. Sandwich it with your thumb as shown above right. Gently squeeze the nippers again and the rectangle will divide into two squares. Making a bridge in this way anticipates the break so that you still have hold of both halves. If you hold only one end of the rectangle, you run the risk of sending squares of glass flying through the air.

To Cut a Tile into Three Long Strips

Sometimes you will want to cut a tile into long thin strips (as in the fins of the Clown Fish Plaque on page 60). To do this, place the nippers one third of the way down and into the tile slightly more than usual, about 8 mm (⅜ in). Gently squeeze as before and your strip should break off. Repeat by breaking the remaining two thirds of the tile in half. If the tile shatters, don't worry, there is always a lot of wastage when cutting strips.

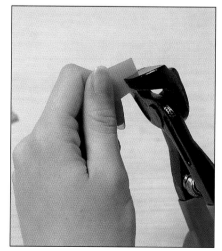

To Cut a Tile into Triangles

Once again, you need to make a bridge of the tile and sandwich it between your thumb, index and middle finger. Place the nippers across the diagonal, about halfway in, and gently squeeze. The tile should divide into two triangles. Sometimes you may find that you are only able to get one successful triangle out of each tile, this is fine. By repeating the process, each one of the large triangles can be split into two smaller ones.

To Cut a Tile into a Circle

Making a circle involves trimming the corners off the tile. The jaws of the nippers are placed entirely across the cutting edge in this case. Keep nibbling until the edges become circular.

To Cut a Mosaic "Eye"

To make the iris, firstly cut a blue (or brown or green) tile into a circle as described above. Then cut it in half and in half again, laying the quarter circles down on the table so that they still fit together. If any of the tesserae shatter, start again. Next, nibble the centre out of each quarter circle. Glue the four pieces back down in their rightful place. Now cut a black tessera for the pupil. Make it small enough to fit inside the iris and glue it in place (see the Clown Fish on page 60).

To Cut a Banana or Crescent Moon Shape

This requires using the "wrong side" of the nippers, that is, the side that doesn't jut out as shown below. Gently squeeze across the tile and if you are lucky you will get a curved cut as opposed to a straight cut. I must admit that even after all these years, this still seems more a matter of luck than judgement, and if I'm doing a demonstration, I can guarantee that it won't work first time!

Once you have managed to cut a curve, you can spin the tile round and cut away from it to create a banana or crescent moon shape as shown in the picture at the bottom. This shape is particularly useful for eyelids (see the Angel Firescreen on page 84) and fish scales .

Where to Begin Mosaicing

If you are a beginner, the temptation is to start with a central feature (e.g. the eye of the Guinea Fowl on page 54). In fact, there are three good reasons why it is best to start with the border:

1 You will gain useful practice at cutting the tiles into tesserae. If a tile cuts at an angle that isn't straight, you can compensate by cutting another to match this angle.

2 Before you mosaic the edge tiles, the work surface has to be completely clean. If there are any glass shards under the board from where you have been cutting, the board will not rest flat. If you mosaic the edge first, before you have done any cutting at all, then there is no need to clear and clean the work surface, it's ready to make a start. Remember to place a sheet of paper or newspaper underneath the MDF panel to prevent it from sticking to the work surface.

3 When the time comes to grout the finished piece, it's the edge tesserae that bear the brunt of the pressure of the grout spreader, if any tesserae are going to fall off it's invariably these. The tiles in the middle have their neighbours to support them, the edge tesserae do not. So if you've mosaiced the edge first, you will be certain that the glue has properly set and that these tesserae are firmly in place.

Having mosaiced the border, you are now ready to start on the design itself. You will soon find that it's much easier to mosaic next to tesserae that have already set. Thus, if you are mosaicing, for example, an eye, it's a good idea to initially place the pupil in position and let it set for half an hour or so (if you are using PVA). When you later add the iris, there is no possibility of the pupil being disturbed. This is only really necessary on very precise areas, such as facial features, where you will want to capture a specific expression and the exact placing of a single tessera can be vital.

Imagine you are mosaicing a fish that is swimming through water. Always mosaic the object that is closest to you **in visual terms** first. This is because, however hard you try, the mosaiced line will never precisely follow your pencil line. If you mosaiced the *opus vermiculatum* (see Glossary) of the background first, this would dictate the outline of the fish, which is obviously more important. Thus, if a fish is swimming through seaweed, the seaweed needs to be worked on first, then the fish and finally the watery background.

TYPES OF MOSAIC

Direct Mosaic

For a direct mosaic, the tesserae are glued directly onto the surface of the piece of wood or pot or whatever it is that you are mosaicing. The pieces are placed the right way up, the uppermost surface becoming the final surface of the finished mosaic. The advantage of working direct is that you can see what you are getting at all stages of the creative process. The resulting mosaic can be transported and exhibited and if you move house you can take it with you. The disadvantage of direct mosaic is that the final surface is not completely flat and is therefore not suitable for floors or other circumstances where a flat surface is required, such as a tabletop or work surface.

A direct mosaic panel on MDF (Medium Density Fibreboard) is not suitable for outdoor use as, in the winter, moisture could soak through the grout and into the MDF and freeze, expand, and thus push the tesserae away from the panel. If an external mosaic is required, then it is recommended that you work "indirect".

Preparation

Before starting to lay tesserae, it is a good idea to cut up a handful of tiles and build up a small reserve to choose from. Place each colour on a piece of paper or a paper plate. Not only will you be able to move each colour close to hand when you need it, but it is also easier to clear away the tesserae by simply inverting the paper and pouring them back into their jar.

It is often said that making a mosaic is like doing a jigsaw puzzle. This is a remark that is guaranteed to infuriate any self-respecting mosaic artist. The fact is that a jigsaw is a puzzle, with a pre-determined solution. No matter how good or bad you are at solving the puzzle, the end result will always be the same. This is certainly not true in mosaic where the result would never be the same and making a mosaic definitely involves a creative process. That said, it is true that when you select a tessera from your pool of tesserae you have to look for the correct shape which has the right angle to the line that you are trying to make and in this respect I agree that it is like doing a jigsaw puzzle.

Make the distance between the pool of tesserae on the paper and the mosaic as short as possible. I actually place the paper on the mosaic, but you may feel that you need to see the entire mosaic at all times. By making the distance short, you can glance from the pool to the mosaic easily and make your selection.

Gluing down Tesserae for a Direct Mosaic

The glue dispenser is designed to release a small quantity of glue at a time, so only cut off the very tip of the nozzle. If you are inexperienced at mosaicing, it can help if you "butter" each tessera individually with a small dab of glue until you become more experienced. As you become more confident you can run a "bead" of glue along the line that you are about to mosaic.

Be generous with the glue, but not to the extent that it squidges out over the top of the tesserae. The adhesive is meant to hold the tesserae in position until you grout the finished mosaic, so you need to ensure that there is still sufficient room for the grout to do its job. Gaps between the tesserae are a necessary part of the mosaic. The gaps, or "interstices" that result when grouted, create the flow or *andamento* of the finished mosaic (see Glossary on page 95). The grout, when set, is very strong and will hold the tesserae in place preventing any side-to-side movement.

Mosaicing a Straight Line of Tesserae

Draw a straight line with a pencil and try to mosaic a line of tesserae along it. You will soon see that it's a bit like steering a car – if you are slightly out at the beginning you don't notice, but a short distance down the road you are driving on the wrong side! Try and "steer" along the line by choosing each successive tessera so that the angle between the line and the previous tessera is the same.

It will soon become apparent that as well as to keep straight the line you are working on, it is equally important to leave yourself a straight line for the next row of tesserae. If a tessera looks good next to its neighbours but juts out below the bottom line, simply nibble it down to the same length. If you don't do this, you can correct things on the next row by placing a thinner tessera next to it, putting yourself back on course. If you don't compensate, you may

well find matters getting progressively worse with each subsequent row.

Mosaicing a Curved Line of Tesserae

If your attempt at a straight line was a success, it was due to the fact that the angles were correct. Indeed, if the sides of the tesserae were all at 90° to the line, you will not have experienced any difficulty; only when the angle varies do you have to choose a tessera with the same angle as the previous one in order to compensate and steer back on course. If the 90° rule applies, then you were simply hitting the line at the perpendicular in each case. The same is true when mosaicing a curved line – if you try to use a tessera with a right angle to the curve each time, then it all becomes much easier. Not surprisingly, what you end up with is a series of wedges which steer themselves round the curve. In this way you can create both concave and convex curves, as shown below, depending on which way up you place the tesserae.

Indirect Mosaic

When you buy a sheet of mosaic tiles, you will see that the tiles are spaced apart, the gap allowing for the grouting. These sheets are usually used for swimming pools. The sheets of tiles are "buttered" with cement and applied to the rendered swimming pool wall. The reverse of the tiles (the face not attached to the paper) is "ribbed" to allow the buttered cement to "key" to them. When dry, the backing paper can be soaked off and the tiles grouted. This is the basic principle of an indirect mosaic.

When a flat surface is required, such as a floor, a tabletop, or a work surface, the mosaic needs to be made indirect. An indirect mosaic requires that the tesserae (vitreous, smalti, pebbles or whatever material you are using) have been laid face-down onto paper using a water-soluble adhesive (e.g. wallpaper paste). Because the surface of the paper is flat, the resultant surface of the mosaic will also be flat. The advantage of working indirect is that the final flat surface is suitable for walls and floors. (It also means that if working on, say, a swimming pool, the mosaic artist can work at home in his warm studio, instead of having to travel to be "on site".) When set into cement or concrete, an indirect mosaic is suitable for external use and will last a lifetime – indeed, if Roman mosaics are an example, for centuries.

Incidentally, there is much debate as to whether the Romans worked indirect or direct. In my opinion, the very reason why Roman mosaics were designed around emblemata (circular pictures in the centre of a larger area containing a background and border) is precisely that the master mosaicist could work in the comfort of his studio on his indirect insertion, whilst the poor apprentices battled it out on their hands and knees working direct.

Working Indirect on a Prepared MDF Board
Paper needs to be stretched over a waxed board as a surface for the tesserae. I have developed this method to prevent the wallpaper glue from sticking the paper to the board, thus making it impossible to remove. Draw a line 5 cm (2 in) all around from the edge of the board. Rub soft beeswax into this internal area (you can rub over it instead, if you wish). Only wax the "mosaic" area; the surround needs to be kept wax-free so the gummed-paper tape will stick to it. You are now ready to stretch your paper.

Stretching a Sheet of Paper
Cut a sheet of paper to stretch onto the board. The sort of paper that is ideal is the thick, brown wrapping paper used in haberdashery shops and hardware stores, called kraft paper. The paper has a smooth side and a ribbed side. Though it is largely a matter of choice, I prefer to lay the "ribbed" side uppermost, so that the tesserae "key" to the paper better. Cut the paper 2 ½ cm (1 in) larger all round than the waxed mosaic area. Tear off four lengths of 5 cm (2 in) wide gummed paper strips from a roll that can be purchased from stationers.

Wet the paper by running it through a bath of cold water; this stretches it. Lay it down in place on the waxed board and fix it with the wetted, gummed-paper strips. As the paper dries, it will shrink and the end result will be that the paper is stretched taut and held down securely on the waxed mosaic board. The waxed board can be reused indefinitely for mosaic items of a similar size.

Gluing down Tesserae for an Indirect Mosaic
Any water-soluble glue or gum can be used. I recommend wallpaper paste as it is cheap and you can mix it to the quantity and viscosity that you prefer. Use the glue sparingly as it only needs to act as a temporary fixing. Too much glue will make the brown paper "buckle", but if you have stretched it properly then the buckling will not be as great. The

paper will shrink back again, but make sure that your tesserae have not been laid too close together, otherwise they will get "scrunched up" against each other when the glue dries and the paper shrinks.

When the indirect mosaic is finished, it is set aside while the surface it is to decorate is prepared with tile adhesive and keyed with a notched trowel (see page 76). The mosaic is cut away from the board and quickly inverted onto the prepared surface. It is then pressed down and left to set. Finally, the paper is soaked off and the piece is grouted in the usual way.

Working Indirect on Sticky-Backed Plastic
Rolls of sticky-backed plastic are available from stationers. Mainly used as a protective waterproof coating for books, maps and other documents, this product is ideally suited to an indirect mosaic where no cutting is required.

The easiest way to work with the plastic is to cut a piece to size, peel it off its backing and let it hang temporarily off the edge of a table. Take the backing sheet and tape it down with the "grid side" up. (A grid is printed on the backing paper to help you cut a straight line.) Now remove the sticky-backed plastic from the table and tape it down sticky-side up. You will be able to use the grid to guide you as you

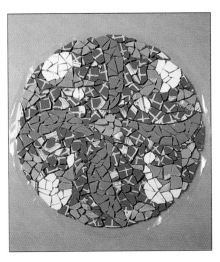

"click" the uncut tiles into place. The mosaic is finished in the same way as for working on MDF board as described above.

The above two photographs show the table top on page 77, first worked indirect on plastic, then inverted onto the prepared table top. The plastic is then peeled off.

I have also made up a few borders to show you how easy and effective this method is (see page 14). Mosaics made in this way can also be incorporated as borders or backgrounds for larger pieces made in the normal indirect way described above.

Grouting
Buy the finest grout available. Powdered grout is available in grey, white, ivory and brown and is also available in a variety of colours "ready-mixed". The ready-mixed grout is fine, but naturally has a shorter shelf-life (this can be greatly improved by cutting out a circular piece of paper and laying it on the surface of the grout that is left in the pot to prevent the air from getting to it and drying it out). Always follow the health and safety instructions on the packet. If you are using

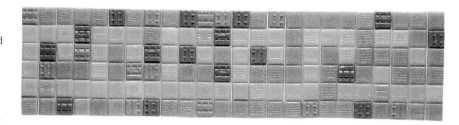

powdered grout, you can colour it at the "dry" stage by adding coloured powder paints and/or up to 50 per cent sand. (Never use sand straight off the beach for building purposes because the salt content is corrosive.) I recommend that you stick to plain grey grout most of the time: the grout delineates the tesserae and it can distract or even overpower the effect of the mosaic tesserae if it is brightly coloured. Occasionally I use brown grout if the overall colour of the mosaic is "warm" and brown seems to be a harmonious choice. I don't use brightly coloured grouts often myself, but I have seen them used to dramatic effect, especially in "jazzy", abstract mosaics.

1 Wearing rubber gloves, pour a mound of the grout onto a flat piece of scrap wood (hardboard is ideal) and make a well in the centre. Gradually add water to the well and mix thoroughly with a small hand trowel. The mixed grout should be of a "mud pie" consistency – if it is too stiff, it won't flow into the gaps, if it is too wet, it will wash out.

2 Starting on the vertical edges, spread the grout with a squeegee or tile grout spreader. Grout the top surface of the mosaic, running the grout spreader across the surface in all directions in order to fill the gaps thoroughly.

3 Wipe the excess grout off the sides and top surface with a damp cloth, working in small circular movements. Rinse the cloth and change the water frequently. Sometimes, in a direct mosaic, a few of the tesserae are set lower than the rest and become submerged by grout: reveal any such tesserae using a penknife or other suitable metal tool. Take some trouble at this stage – it is much harder to remove grout once it has set.

4 The drying of the grout is a chemical process and takes about 24 hours; placing the mosaic in the hot sun will not speed up the drying time. You can place a damp towel over the grouted mosaic for 24 hours to create a damp environment and let the grout set more slowly.

5 The finished mosaic lacks some of the shine that it had before it was grouted. This is partially due to an unavoidable scum of grout remaining on the surface. After a day or so when the grout has set, give the mosaic a scrub with a liquid floor cleaner using an abrasive sponge pad.

6 If you are making a direct mosaic plaque, screw D rings or mirror plates to the back and hang it in a place that allows the light to play on the surface and shows it off to best effect.

Right: A selection of borders worked indirect onto sticky-backed plastic ready to be inverted onto the prepared design surface.

14

DESIGNING

Keep your design simple and uncluttered. Make sure that you have a strong tonal contrast between the subject (fish, bird, etc.) and the background, so that the subject stands out visually, even from a distance.

Dividing up Shapes into Key Lines

Even with the simplest of shapes, there is a choice to be made as to how to mosaic them. Consider the leaf outline shown above right. The most naturalistic way to tackle it is to divide it into two with a central line and use that to "cast off" from as you work your way upwards to the tip of the leaf. Another solution is to mosaic an outer row, then work inwards. This choice has the advantage of making sure that the outline of the leaf is clean and well-defined. Another option is to work curves from both sides. Although not as realistic as the first option, this can still be effective. The finished effect in mosaic is shown beside the diagrams.

Background *Opus*

Consider the Flower Hot Plate (right). The order of working is first the central image, then the border, then the *opus vermiculatum* (see page 96). Note how the *opus vermiculatum* emphasizes the shape of the central image, while at the same time rounding off the sharp points.

This leaves the background. There are many ways in which to mosaic the background. A simple solution is to work in straight vertical or horizontal lines, as in the Indian Elephant Tea Tray (page 66). Vertical lines tend to stretch an object, horizontal ones tend to condense it.

Alternatively, you could consider the "line of action", as for the fish (page 60). Draw it onto your design and echo it with parallel lines working outwards to the edge of the mosaic. It is important to concentrate on the line of action only. In other words, you must "crash through" the reeds, but this will be fine because the *opus vermiculatum* is there to act as a barrier between the background line of flow and those of the fish itself. This is known as *opus musivum* and literally means "pertaining to the muses", so already we are looking at something that conveys a thinking process rather than a simply mechanical one. For me, this is the most effective and attractive of all the different *opuses*.

Opus musivum works best when there is a single object, as in the Guinea Fowl project on page 54. If there are lots of objects, it isn't possible to distinguish a line of flow. The horizontal *opus regulatum* is essential in such a case, to calm down a busy subject.

Studio Set-up

Obviously the ideal set-up is to have a room set aside which is completely devoted to your mosaic activity. (This is commonly known a the "mosaic studio".) However, for the beginner at least, this is hardly likely to be the case. Choose a room with plenty of natural light, good ventilation and, if possible, uncarpeted – it's much easier to sweep up than to vacuum the carpet at the end of each mosaic session. It's useful to have a wall on which to pin your designs for viewing from a distance and to put up shelves on which to store the various materials.

1 PROJECT

Cheeky Raku Tile

Designer and maker: Martin Cheek

his simple project uses the subtle colour variations in smalti to create a mosaic border which will enhance the intrinsic beauty of a hand-made or purchased tile. It tips a wink at the greatest Impressionist of them all, Georges Seurat. He painted like a mosaic artist works, using the direction of his dots of paint to suggest movement. In his pointillist borders the dots fuse together with great subtlety to suggest a light source shining on the painting itself.

You will need

36 pieces of smalti of your own colour choice are required to frame a 15 cm (6 in) tile

Ruler
Sharp pencil
Sheets of newspaper
MDF, 10 mm (⅜ in) thick, approx. 1.5 cm (½ in) wider all round than the dimensions of the tile
125 ml (4 fl oz) wood adhesive in a dispenser
Glazed tile
Safety spectacles
Face mask
Mosaic nippers
Smalti, as shown above
Black paint or ink
Brush to apply colour
Rubber gloves
450 g (1 lb) powdered grout
Bowl of water
Mixing board for the grout
Stick to mix the grout
Plastic grout spreader
Cleaning cloth
Liquid floor cleaner
Abrasive cleaning pad

1 Using a ruler, draw diagonal lines from corner to corner on the MDF. Glue the tile down, so that each corner touches a diagonal line. My tile, being hand-made, was not exactly square, so a compromise was reached.

2 Before gluing down any tesserae, arrange the various shades around the tile. I find it helpful to establish a light source, in this case the top left corner, and gradually darken the colours as I work to (in this case) the bottom right corner.

3 When you are happy with the effect, run a bead of glue down each side of the MDF and apply the smalti. You may need to trim a tessera on each side to achieve a snug fit. If this is the case, it is less noticeable to trim one of the middle tesserae rather than one of the corner ones. Allow the glue to set.

artist's tip
Grouting smalti when you have been working direct can be time-consuming due to the uneven surface. The grout will fill any air bubbles in the surface of the smalti – you do not need to pick it out as this is considered an intrinsic part of this hand-made material.

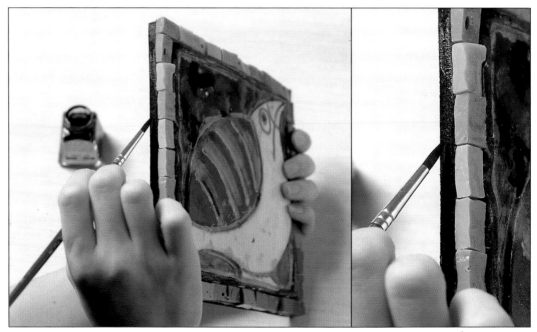

4 Paint the edge of the MDF black. If you use ink, it actually stains into the MDF, which means that, if you are careful, you don't need to touch the smalti with the paintbrush at all.

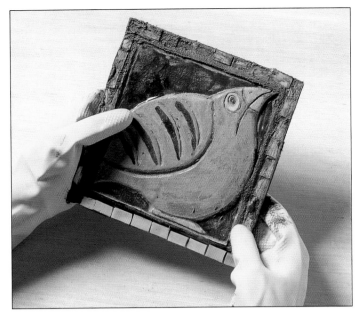

5 Grout the tile if you wish. If you have worked tight enough with the mosaic, then it isn't really necessary to grout at all. I have made one tile with grout (the yellow bird below) and one without (shown on page 16), so that you can decide for yourself which you think looks best.

Alternative designs:

Cheeky birds

Designer and maker: Martin Cheek

I've chosen another bird, this time one with warm colours (above and below left), to show you an alternative. Pick out the part of the tile that you want to emphasize (I have chosen the bright yellow beak) and use various shades of that colour for the smalti border. I would rarely choose the dominant colour from the tile (the dark blue background) but would pick a colour to harmonize with it.

The crested bird (below right) is framed using 2 cm (¾ in) square vitreous tiles. I like to alternate veined with unveined tiles to add texture. Working from the corners inwards, uncut tiles are used until you get to the middle where three tiles are divided to fill the remaining space.

Jazzy Mirror

Designer and maker: Kerry Balman

W̶e wanted to include a project that involved hardly any cutting at all. Gold leaf smalti is real gold leaf sandwiched in glass and is used to fabulous effect in Byzantine churches: St Mark's in Venice has glorious examples. Not surprisingly, it is very expensive. Our solution was to "dilute" it with gold mirror. The contrast between the reflective gold mirror and the non-reflective gold leaf smalti adds to the three-dimensional quality of this piece. If you decide to use only pre-cut gold leaf smalti, the project can be achieved with no cutting whatsoever.

You will need

69 gold leaf smalti pieces as shown above
109 pieces of gold mirror as shown above, in strips

Safety spectacles
Face mask
Mosaic nippers
Sheets of newspaper
MDF mirror blank (see Suppliers), surround painted dark blue
125 ml (4 fl oz) wood adhesive in a dispenser
Metal modelling tool or cocktail stick
Gold ink
Soft paintbrush

1 The gold leaf smalti can be bought pre-cut into 1 cm (⅜ in) squares but it is more economical to buy it in 1 cm (⅜ in) strips. Cutting the strips into 1 cm (⅜ in) tesserae requires very little effort and is soon done. Note: wearing a pair of goggles is particularly important when working with mirror, which can shatter.

2 The whole fun of this project lies in simply arranging the gold leaf smalti and gold mirror, randomly mixed, into shapes that please you. Enjoy yourself and start to play with the tesserae, creating swirling lines on the mirror surround, without using any glue at this stage.

3 Continuing the lines visually "through" the mirror will give your design a sense of unity. It may help to begin with the centre top of the mirror frame, then place an arrangement on either side in the centre before working the two bottom corners and finally filling the areas in between.

4 When you are happy with the effect that you have created, stick the tesserae down. The cleanest way to do this is to have a pool of glue in a container and dab a little glue onto the back of each tesserae with a metal modelling tool or cocktail stick. Apply the smallest amount of glue possible in order to prevent it from squeezing over the edges. Allow the glue to set before you continue.

5 Using a small brush, paint the fluting on the surround with gold ink to finish the mirror. Hold the frame from underneath, so that you don't smudge the wet paint. Wait until completely dry before fitting the mirror glass.

making mosaics/project 2

3 PROJECT Golden Key Holder

Designer: Martin Cheek   Maker: Kerry Balman

This simple key design gives practice in cutting gold mirror and arranging the pieces elegantly in a defined space. Alternative arrangements with found objects show more elaborate treatments of this shape. Buttons, beads and shells are a useful source to the mosaic artist as they are available in an amazing range of colours, sizes and materials. When using found objects for mosaic, the same design considerations apply: try to achieve contrast in the various tones, shapes, sizes and materials that you use. Make sure that your motifs, however simple (as in the flowers shown in the examples here), are clearly defined and stand out from the secondary or background designs.

You will need

53 pieces of gold mirror

Green acrylic paint
Artist's paintbrush
Sheets of newspaper
MDF key holder blank, ready for
painting (see Suppliers)
Gold ink
Tracing paper
Sharp pencil
Sheet of paper
Gold mirror, as shown above
Safety spectacles
Face mask
Mosaic nippers
Metal modelling tool or
cocktail stick
125 ml (4 fl oz) wood adhesive
in a dispenser

1   Begin by painting the background. I tend to apply a dark first coat, then "dry brush" the highlights when this is dry. Keep going until you are happy with the texture of the green. Leave to dry. Carefully paint the MDF fluting with gold ink.

2 So as not to spoil your paintwork, it is worth drawing the key design on a separate piece of paper. Trace the template on page 92, then enlarge it on a photocopier to the correct size for your key holder. Transfer the exact position of the screw holes to the design, then mark where you will place the hooks for the keys.

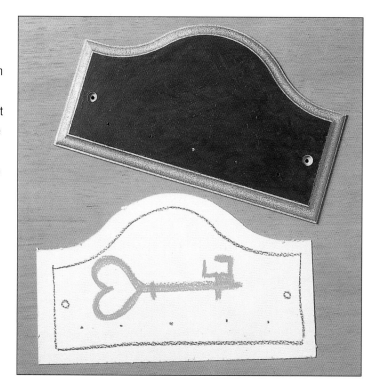

3 You need to see the entire key mosaiced to be sure that it is looking good before gluing it down onto the MDF. Nibble the gold mirror tiles into shape and lay them out on your paper template. How the key sits on the background is very important, so this is a way of getting the proportions right without having to worry about the paint finish.

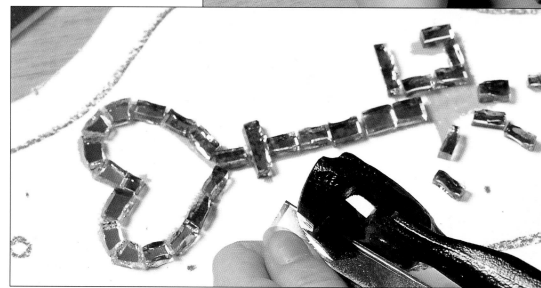

4 When you are happy with the design of the key, transfer it carefully, one tessera at a time, to the MDF. Start with the pieces in the centre of the design and work outwards on either side. You may need to adjust the positions to ensure that the pieces fit comfortably between the border and the hook points.

artist's tip
Try not to use too much glue as it will squidge out and spoil the paintwork. If this happens, wipe it off immediately with a cocktail stick or a piece of tissue paper.

5 Once all the tesserae of the design have been placed in the correct positions, pick up individual tesserae and butter with a minimum amount of glue using a metal modelling tool or cocktail stick.

4 PROJECT Windmill Placemat

Designer: Martin Cheek   Maker: Laura Elson

T his simple two-colour design is reminiscent of the Dutch "Delft" style. If you already have Delft tiles or tableware in your kitchen, this placemat (or set of placemats if you make more) will be an attractive addition to your collection.

1 Enlarge the template on page 92 on a photocopier to the correct size for your placemat, then transfer the design to the mat using carbon paper. Colour in the design with the crayons or pencils. Begin by mosaicing the blue border. Although this is a relatively easy project, the wavy lines will give you good practice in mosaicing concave and convex curves. Try to keep inside the inner line created by the edge of the fluting in order to avoid having sharp points around the edge of the mosaic.

2 When mosaicing the blue sails, start with their outlines, then fill them in, to achieve a clean result.

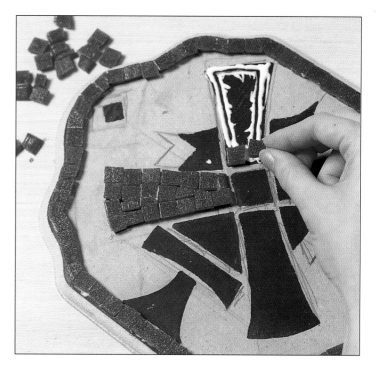

3 When you have finished all four sails, mosaic a white line along the sides of each one, separating the sails from the mill design.

4 Mosaic the rest of the windmill. You can clearly see the original guide line, which I altered when I filled in the design. I left the line visible so that you can see how, even on such a basic shape, a small change can make all the difference.

5 The outline of mosaic around the subject is known as the *opus vermiculatum*. This close-up shows how you will have to nibble down the basic quarter-tile tesserae in order to achieve a neat result in the sharp angles.

6 Continue with the *opus vermiculatum* until you have worked all round the windmill. Mosaic a circle of white around each of the two blue tiles on either side of the windmill.

7 You can use tweezers to position very small pieces of nibbled tesserae. Mosaic the background with lines of tesserae radiating out to meet the border. Allow the glue to set and grout your mosaic in the normal way.

Gallery One

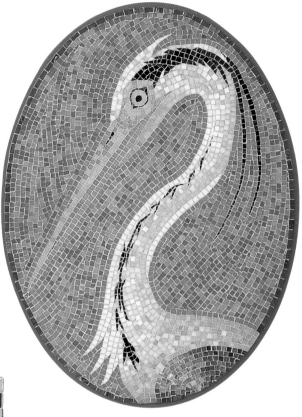

Heron #2
Designer: Martin Cheek
Maker: Danny Branscombe Kent
Medium: Vitreous Glass
Size: 82 x 62 cm (32¼ x 24½ in)
Date: 1999

This piece was commissioned by Kent County Council as part of their Mobile Arts Unit to be hired out by local schools. I wanted to demonstrate how even a simple shape when mosaiced can be sufficient, and I like the way that this piece also works as a "close up" of the heron shown on page 7.

The large, dagger-shaped bill of the heron is a gift to the mosaic artist, offering a thrust of bright colour. I also wanted to make a feature of the two black strands which hang down behind the head. These are echoed in the little white quiff on the top of the head and also in the line of the three points that brush out at the base of his neck.

Siberian Crane
Designer and maker: Martin Cheek
Medium: Vitreous Glass
Size: 30 x 30 cm (12 x 12 in)
Date: 1998

I am slowly working towards making my work simpler and hopefully less fussy. This whole piece is about the line of the Crane's neck which is echoed throughout the background in *opus musivum*. I like the freshness of these particular blues, they remind me of the sky in India on the day when I was lucky enough to see the now rare sight of a pair of Siberian cranes.

Fish
Designer and maker: Jo Letchford
Medium: Vitreous glass, Cinca ceramic and mirror
Size: 22 x 31 cm (8¾ x 12¼ in)
Date: 1998

This fish is inspired by a similar fish included in a large Roman mosaic floor from Pompeii. Using the non-reflective Cinca ceramic for the fish, so that the sea of vitreous glass and mirror shines out, is very effective here.

Duck

Designer and maker: Emma Abel
Medium: Ceramic
Size: 28 x 30 cm (11 x 12 in)
Date: 1999

This cheerful duck is defined by a simple outline as opposed to a silhouette. I like the way that the feet are visible beneath the surface adding a touch of whimsy to this piece. Once again, it is easy to imagine this piece being one of a set.

Tea Pot

Designer and maker: Emma Ropner
Medium: Vitreous glass and gold leaf smalti
Size: 15 cm (6 in) square
Date: 1998

This little piece is ideally suited to be used as a coaster. Emma's gay style has a naïve charm to it reminiscent of children's drawings.

Red Pepper

Designer and maker: Jo Letchford
Medium: Vitreous glass
Size: 19 x 21 cm (7½ x 8¼ in)
Date: 1998

Jo mosaiced this pepper from life whilst on my mosaic course in Greece. She picked a pepper from the vegetable patch outside the studio, sliced it in half and that was all the inspiration she needed to make this mosaic. It's interesting to note that the lime green "inner pepper" would not have been included if this mosaic had not been drawn from life.

Sea Turtle

Designer and maker: Alison Slater (Zantium)
Medium: Vitreous glass and smalti
Size: 33 x 33 cm (13 x 13 in)
Date: 1997

Because this mosaic was made as an indirect slab, it was possible to mix the smalti in with the vitreous glass. I like the way that Alison has incorporated lime green markings into the red and brown shell in order to visually link it with the rest of the turtle. The use of *opus musivum* for the background helps to create the illusion of movement through the water.

Tree-of-life Cachepot

Designer and maker: Maria Starling

T he designer's strong sense of pattern and colour is evident in this project. Abstract in nature, the tree also suggests a joyous dancing figure. Its celebratory quality reminds me of the later "cut outs" of Henri Matisse.

You will need

16 light blue, 98 dark blue, 169 light green and 73 dark vermilion vitreous glass tiles

Sheet of A4 carbon paper
Tracing paper
Sharp pencil
Sheets of newspaper
MDF cachepot blank, ready for painting (see Suppliers)
Crayons or coloured pencils
Various vitreous glass tiles, as shown above
Safety spectacles
Face mask
Mosaic nippers
125 ml (4 fl oz) wood adhesive in a dispenser
Rubber gloves
450 g (1 lb) of powdered grout
Bowl of water
Mixing board for the grout
Stick to mix the grout
Plastic grout spreader
Cleaning cloth
Liquid floor cleaner
Abrasive cleaning pad

1 Enlarge the template on page 93 on a photocopier to the correct size for your cachepot, then transfer the design to the pot using carbon paper. Colour it in so that you only have to worry about the actual mosaicing. On a simple design like this, neatness is essential if the design is to work. Remember that "simple" doesn't mean "easy".

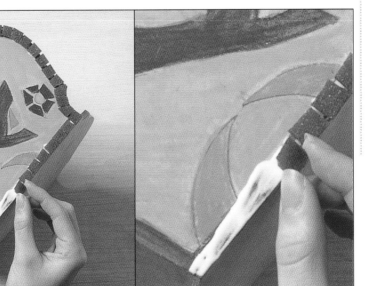

2 Because the cachepot is tapered it helps if you prop it up so that the surface you are working on is horizontal. Mosaic the top and sides of the border, being careful not to go over the edge of the MDF, as shown. Allow the glue to set.

3 Place the cachepot on its base to mosaic the base line. This will ensure that no tesserae stick over the base and cause the cachepot to wobble. Allow the glue to set.

4 Mosaic the tree. Try to work neatly here in order to get clean flowing lines. The tree is the focus of attention and therefore the most important element of this piece.

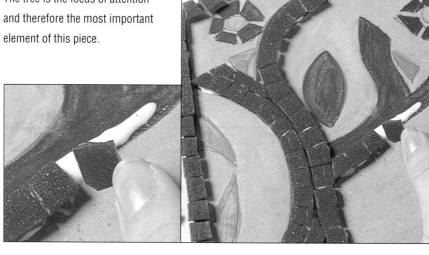

5 The pale blue leaves are next. Even though each leaf consists of only three tesserae, try to achieve a clean overall shape. The flowers in the top right and left corners of the design are made by placing carefully cut wedges together to form a circle (see step 6).

6 The background here echoes the flow of the various elements. As already noted, the tree is the most important element, so it has dominance when it comes to mosaicing the background. Notice how the lines of mosaic around the tree take precedence over the work around the leaves and flowers. When you have finished this side, leave the glue to set. Repeat on the other three sides of the cachepot. When completed, grout in the usual way.

Alternative design:
Celtic Knot

Designer and maker:
Danny Branscombe Kent

Taking this simple knot and linking it around each side of the cachepot is an inspirational idea. Changing the colourways on each side adds to the three-dimensionality of the piece. The skill here is in trying to ensure that the bands visually appear to continue on neatly as they intertwine.

6 PROJECT Crazy Concrete Planter

Designer and maker: Kerry Balman

Do you have a collection of valuable family china that has accidentally been broken over the years but that you have never had the heart to throw away? If so, it's probably stacked away in your attic somewhere, waiting for that day when you can decide what to do with it. Well, here is the ideal solution – use the pieces to make a mosaic planter!

You will need

Broken tiles and china in a range of tones and colours

Concrete planter, bought from any garden centre
4 cut-outs, one for each side
1 kg (2.2 lb) ready-mixed or powdered tile adhesive suitable for exterior use
Plastic mixing bowl or basin
Spoon to mix the adhesive
Putty knife
Pieces of broken tiles and china
Safety spectacles
Face mask
Mosaic nippers
Rubber gloves
450 g (1 lb) powdered grout
Bowl of water
Mixing board for the grout
Stick to mix the grout
Cleaning cloth
Liquid floor cleaner
Abrasive cleaning pad
Blue stain (optional)
Small household brush to apply stain (optional)
Coloured cement pigment (optional)

1 I think that pieces like this, even though "crazy", still work best if they have a focal point. On this side we decided on a central focus of a cut-out sea horse. Stick this down using the exterior tile adhesive, mixed according to the manufacturer's instructions. The easiest way to fix each piece is to "butter" it with a putty knife.

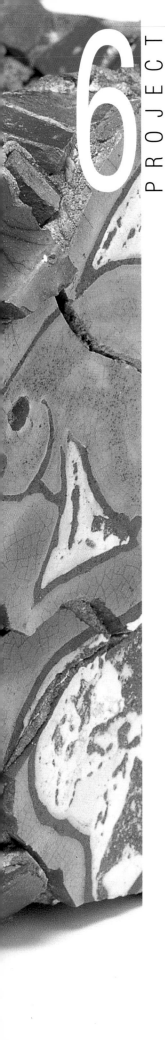
2 Our planter had been cast to incorporate a brick wall effect. Filling in the "mortar lines" with the adhesive helped to create a smoother surface. Start by working with the larger pieces and gradually work your way down in scale. Use your nippers to trim any projecting pieces and to shape where necessary. We were lucky enough to have some broken, curved tesserae which exactly matched the curve of the planter.

3 Continue working outwards from the central motif until you have entirely covered the surface and the rim. Mosaic the other three sides of the planter in the same way.

4 Mosaic the inside of the planter down to where the earth will reach.

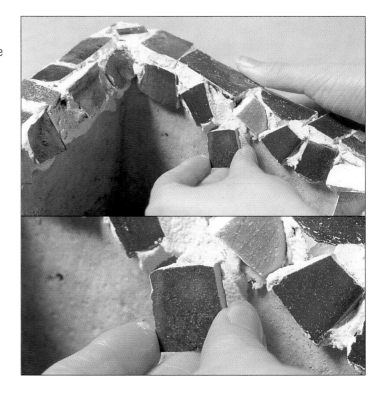

5 If you have used sufficient adhesive, the excess will fill in any gaps and you will not need to grout your planter. If you do decide to grout, you probably won't be able to use a grout spreader due to the unevenness of the mosaiced surface. Instead smear the grout into the gaps with your fingers – wearing rubber gloves of course! When we had finished we felt that the white adhesive looked very stark so we decided to stain it blue to harmonize with the mosaic. Alternatively, you could colour the grout before applying it.

6 Clean off the stain from the surface of the mosaic with a damp cloth and leave to dry.

artist's tip
Whether a piece like this works or not depends entirely on the colour sense of the artist. Achieving an interesting range of tone and colour is essential if the piece is not to appear flat and bland. Your assortment of broken tiles, crockery and china will be different from ours. The beauty of a project like this lies in the uniqueness of your personal collection. If you are unsure about how to go about this project, one solution is to start with large pieces that are light in tone. Gradually darken the tone as the pieces reduce in size. Use the darkest, smallest pieces to fill in any remaining gaps.

Harlequin Box

Designer and maker: Kerry Balman

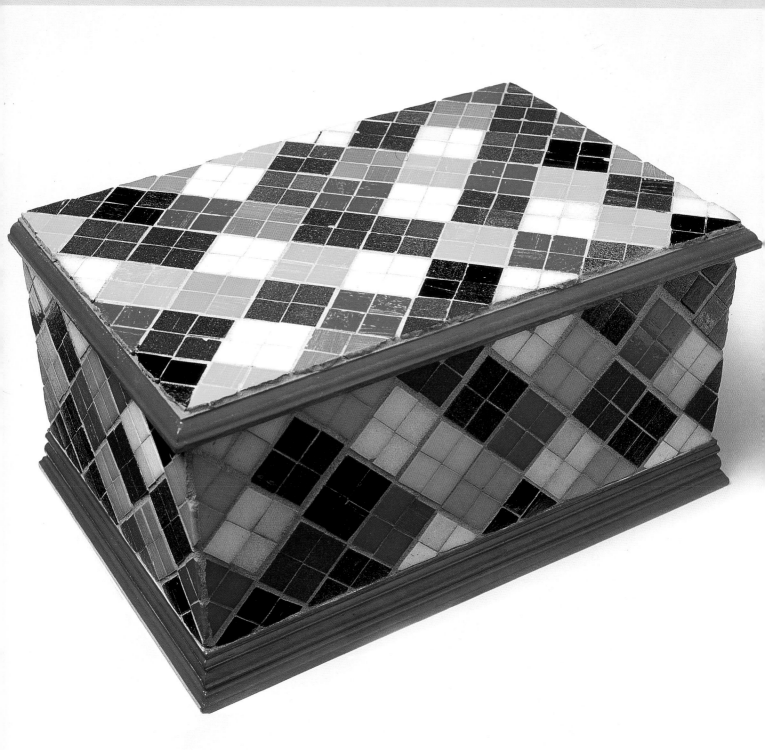

This project is relatively easy as it requires very little cutting. The bold harlequin design is effective due to the strong bold colours. Obviously you can choose them to fit in with the harlequin box's environment. A matching "Pierrot" box can be made using only black and white tiles. If you normally buy your vitreous tiles in a loose mixed box, you inevitably end up with lots of left-over tiles (usually blues and whites). This box is an excellent way to use up the excess, so that you needn't feel guilty about buying a new batch of mix! If your blank box is the same as the one we used, you will be able to follow the design exactly. If not, you will need to adapt the dimensions of the pattern to suit your box.

You will need

Vitreous glass tiles of your own colour choice

60 cm (24 in) steel ruler
Pencil or crayon
Sheets of newspaper
MDF box blank, ready for painting (see Suppliers)
Vitreous glass tiles, as shown above
Safety spectacles
Face mask
Mosaic nippers
125 ml (4 fl oz) wood adhesive in a dispenser
Rubber gloves
450 g (1 lb) powdered grout
Bowl of water
Mixing board for the grout
Stick to mix the grout
Plastic grout spreader
Cleaning cloth
Liquid floor cleaner
Abrasive cleaning pad

1 Draw a diagonal grid on the box to ensure that the tiles will be evenly spaced and symmetrical. Our box was an exact fit from top to bottom but slightly too long from left to right, so we had to tweak the squares apart evenly in the east–west direction to make the grid look visually correct. We have chosen to use squares consisting of four tiles each, but if your box is bigger, e.g. a blanket box, nine-tile squares may be more appropriate.

2 Mosaic the first diagonal line of tiles on the lid. The neater you can be at this point the better – any discrepancy will be compounded as you continue to work outwards. I think it looks nicer if you don't have a repeat pattern of colours; keeping their positioning random will give a more authentic "harlequin" feel to the finished box.

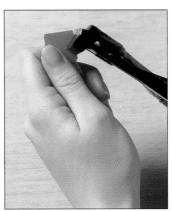

3 When you come to the edge of the box you will need to cut triangles. It is almost impossible to get two large triangles from one tile, so my advice is not to try. Instead "creep up" on the triangle by cutting almost at the diagonal, then

trimming both ends of the hypotenuse to a straight line. Use a complete tile to "buffer" the triangular tesserae to the edge (see page 49, step 5). Cut tiles can scratch so it is important that any overhanging corners and edges are trimmed flush with the edge of the box.

4 Continue adding diagonal lines until you have covered the lid.

5 When stretching the design in the east–west or north-south direction, leave a little more space between the coloured squares, but keep the tiles within each square close together, as shown here.

6 Mosaic the sides of the box. Notice how the colour of each square on the edge of the lid visually continues over the side. You can get away with a slightly wider gap at the top because of the overhang of the lid. Leave the glue to set and grout in the normal way. The gaps in the east–west direction are not so noticeable once the box has been grouted.

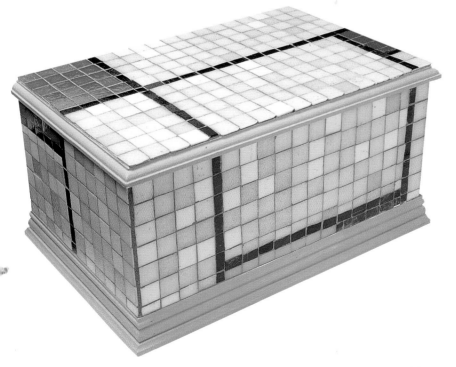

Alternative design:
Mondrian Box

Designer and maker: Martin Cheek

This design is based on the 1929 painting *Composition* by the Constructivist painter Piet Mondrian. His linear style translates perfectly to mosaic. Even though white tiles dominate the piece, I still decided to use grey grout because it delineates the white tiles and emphasizes that this is in fact a mosaic and not simply a painted box. It's also interesting to note that the largest quantity of tiles does not produce the dominant colour – note how the band of yellow, for example, which contains the fewest tesserae (seven) sings out from the rest of the piece.

making mosaics/project 7   45

Jewellery Box

Designer and maker: Emma Abel

like the way the design of this box works from all sides. There is a playful sense of flowers growing up the sides and over onto the lid reminiscent of a clinging vine. The flowers look bright and fresh, and making them out of shiny glass tesserae against a matt ceramic background reinforces this effect. The box looks remarkably colourful, despite the fact that only three colours of tile plus the regal reddish-pink paintwork are used.

You will need

30 green and 50 turquoise vitreous glass tiles
95 cream ceramic mosaic tiles

Sheet of carbon paper
Tracing paper
Sharp pencil
Crayons or coloured pencils
Sheets of newspaper
MDF jewellery box blank, ready for painting (see Suppliers)
Vitreous glass tiles as shown above
Safety spectacles
Face mask
Mosaic nippers
125 ml (4 fl oz) wood adhesive in a dispenser
Metal modelling tool or cocktail stick
Ceramic mosaic tiles, as shown above
Rubber gloves
450 g (1 lb) powdered grout
Bowl of water
Mixing board for the grout
Stick to mix the grout
Plastic grout spreader
Cleaning cloth
Liquid floor cleaner
Abrasive cleaning pad
Red and green paint
Paintbrush

1 Enlarge the templates on page 93 on a photocopier to the size of your box, then transfer the design to the box using carbon paper. Make sure the stems line up visually as they continue over the lid to the sides of the box. As always, it is worth colouring in the design for the sake of clarity.

2 Cut the tesserae for each entire flower, then stick them down on the lid. A metal modelling tool or cocktail stick will help with fine positioning.

3 Finish mosaicing the lid with the ceramic tiles, adding in the peppering of lime green tesserae randomly as you work. As well as tying the design together, this also helps to break up the flatness of the ceramic background. Set aside to dry.

4 Mosaic the side of the box, making sure that the flower stem joins up visually with the one on the lid. Allow the glue to set thoroughly, then mosaic the other side.

5 The ceramic tiles aren't bevelled like the vitreous ones, so it is easier to get a neat edging. Use a spare tile as a buffer as shown to make sure that the tesserae are lined up neatly and evenly with the edge of the box.

6 Work on one end of the box in a similar way. Allow the glue to set thoroughly before mosaicing the opposite end of the box. Finally, grout in the normal way, then paint the edges of the box, taking care not to get paint on the mosaic tiles.

9 PROJECT
Flower Hot Plate

Designer and maker: Danny Branscombe Kent

This design is inspired by a detail from a stained glass window in Flint House. The detail was 10 cm (4 in) in diameter and demonstrates how even such a simple motif as this primrose can make an interesting and attractive mosaic.

You will need

90 white and 24 raw sienna
ceramic mosaic tiles
45 yellow and 37 fawn
vitreous glass tiles

2 sheets of A4 carbon paper
Tracing paper
Sharp pencil
Sheets of newspaper
30 cm (12 in) MDF placemat (see
Suppliers)
Crayons or coloured pencils
Vitreous glass tiles, as shown
above
Safety spectacles
Face mask
Mosaic nippers
125 ml (4 fl oz) wood adhesive in
a dispenser
Ceramic tiles, as shown above
Rubber gloves
450 g (1 lb) powdered grout
Bowl of water
Mixing board for the grout
Stick to mix the grout
Plastic grout spreader
Cleaning cloth
Liquid floor cleaner
Abrasive cleaning pad

1 Enlarge the template on page 90 on a photocopier to the size of your placemat, then transfer the design to the mat using carbon paper. Colour in the design. Begin by mosaicing one of the leaves and move on to the insides of the petals. Try to visualize each leaf in terms of key lines.

2 Draw on the lines of the *opus* as a guide. Mosaic all the areas of fawn first.

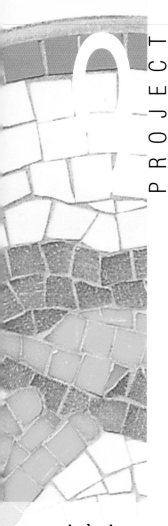

3 Notice how the yellow tesserae continue the *opus* of the fawn ones at the base of the leaf, but not so at the top of it. This is because the actual concave modelling of the leaf has been taken into account.

4 Once you have completed the flower, add the rim using the ceramic tiles. Make sure you create a neat edge.

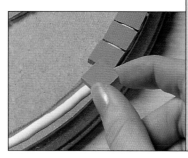

artist's tip

When mosaicing the *opus vermiculatum* (step 5), start in the centre of a straight line in order to practise and get into the swing of it and to build up your confidence before you tackle the more difficult task of going round corners.

5 Now begin working on the *opus vermiculatum*. This detail clearly shows how it "softens" the sharp points within the subject. This pointed tip has been mosaiced around to create a smooth curve, so that when the background of concentric circles "crashes" into it, it will look neat.

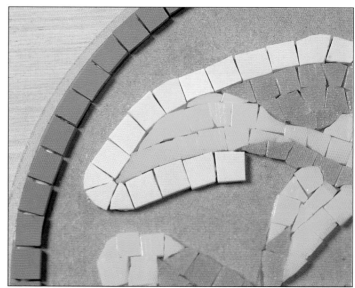

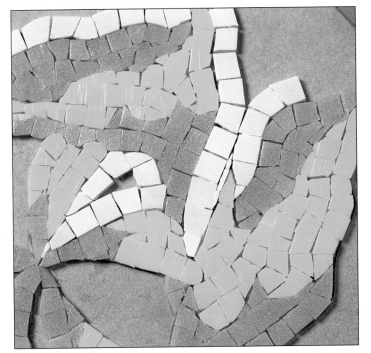

Seal and Anubis

Designer: Martin Cheek

Makers: Kerry Balman and Laura Elson

This non-traditional approach defies all the teachings of the Roman style of mosaic-making which employs the various *opuses* described elsewhere in this book. This "crazy paving" style of mosaic-making depends entirely on creating a really strong, well-defined silhouette. Although the mosaic is haphazard, the carefully worked outline of the subject still makes it effective.

6 The *opus vermiculatum* even exists in the small areas. Clean, smooth lines, as shown here, will enhance the finished effect. Note how the matt surface of the ceramic tiles recedes visually, allowing the shiny flower to stand out.

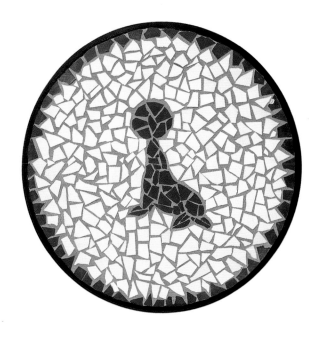

7 Working from the outside inwards, mosaic concentric circles to complete the mosaic. Add pencil guidelines to help with the positioning. Leave to dry, then grout in the usual way.

making mosaics/project 9

This design is a modern interpretation of a Roman mosaic I came across in Cyprus. It is executed in ceramic mosaic tiles which have a matt finish and muted colours, suggesting the subtle texture of natural stone.

This design is a modern interpretation of a Roman mosaic I came across in Cyprus. It is executed in ceramic mosaic tiles which have a matt finish and muted colours, suggesting the subtle texture of natural stone.

You will need

1 branko (white), 12 granite brown, 24 yellow, 88 red, 40 light blue, 64 dark cream, 7 granite red and 24 black ceramic mosaic tiles

Sheet of A4 carbon paper
Tracing paper
Sharp pencil
Sheets of newspaper
MDF, 18 mm (⅝ in) thick, approx. 30 x 30 cm (12 x 12 in)
Crayons or coloured pencils
Ceramic mosaic tiles, as shown above
Safety spectacles
Face mask
Mosaic nippers
125 ml (4 fl oz) wood adhesive in a dispenser
Rubber gloves
450 g (1 lb) powdered grout
Metal tool to spread adhesive
Bowl of water
Mixing board for the grout
Stick to mix the grout
Plastic grout spreader
Cleaning cloth
Liquid floor cleaner
Abrasive cleaning pad
Pair of D rings with screws to hang your finished mosaic

1 Enlarge the template on page 91 on a photocopier to the size of your MDF board, then transfer the design to the board using carbon paper. Colour in the design. Mosaic the vertical sides of the board first, then the geometric border. If the glued tesserae on the side haven't set yet, be careful not to disturb any of them by pushing too hard with the ones on the outer row of the border. For the geometric border to work it is essential that you have 23 tesserae on each side, i.e. a total of 88 tesserae (you only count the corner ones once). Use neatly cut quarter-tile tesserae, and if you can get them evenly spaced, it will greatly help you later in the project.

2 Keep working inwards with the border, changing the colour from cream to brown when necessary. Because the ceramic tesserae are flat on both sides, they require less glue than vitreous glass. Either lay a bead of glue or use a metal tool to "butter" each tessera with glue.

3 First, nibble the branko (white) tile to a circular shape for the eye and glue it down. To nibble the inverted curves for the beak and crop details, use the "wrong" edge of the jaws of the nippers. This may take a few attempts. Offer the cut shapes up to the design to see if you are satisfied before sticking them down.

4 Because the outline shape of the bird is important, it helps to work from the outside in. If the remaining inner space turns out to be slightly different from the template, it won't matter too much, so long as the overall shape is good.

5 Continue to mosaic the bird's speckled feathers, spiralling in as you work.

artist's tip

You can see just how helpful it can be to colour in your design if you compare step 1 to the black and white template on page 91. All the differently coloured feathers, which are a great feature of this design, look really confusing before they are coloured in.

6 Mosaic the feet. For each foot, work on the key line, which is the leg continuing down to the central claw, then add the other claws. These require careful nibbling to get the shape of the claws right.

7 With the bird completed, it is now time to work on the *opus vermiculatum*. Round off any sharp points, like the claws, so that the background has a smooth rhythm to it.

8 The background work within the inner square is known as *opus musivum*. It contrasts well with the ordered regularity of the geometric border. Grout in the normal way. Screw the "D" rings to the back of the board to hang the picture.

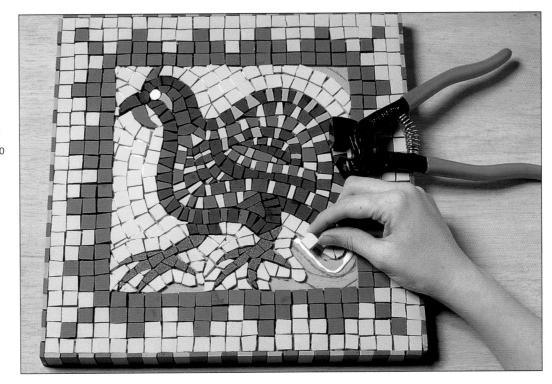

Gallery Two

Arab Mosque
Designer and maker: Collette Price
Medium: Cinca ceramic and vitreous glass
Size: 36 x 18 cm (14 x 7 in)
Date: 1998

Collette lived for a long time in Dubai. The old adage of "write about what you know" can equally well be applied to mosaic. This piece perfectly recaptures that feeling of walking out into the warm light from a dark, cool interior. The use of non-reflective flat ceramic to depict the interior arch which, in turn, frames the shiny vitreous glass exterior scene has never been better employed.

Indian Bird
Designer and maker: Martin Cheek
Medium: Vitreous Glass
Size: 30 x 30 cm (12 x 12 in)
Date: 1998

Another light-hearted bird. These birds cheer up my studio (and me) and that is my excuse for keeping on making them. The subtle pink, green and blue in the vitreous range which seem so uninspiring when seen on a colour chart next to the brighter colours, are extremely useful for backgrounds, as clearly demonstrated here.

Spice Rack
Designer and maker: Emma Abel
Medium: Broken tiles
Size: 21 x 34 x 16 cm (8¼ x 13½ x 6¼ in)
Date: 1998

Emma's style is very much suited to the dazzling use of broken china and tiles. The hot, fiery colours employed here serve as a reminder to use those spices with caution!

Grecian Urn

Designer: Martin Cheek
Maker: Kerry Balman
Medium: Cinca ceramic
Size: 20 cm (8 in) square
Date: 1999

Even a simple graphic motif like this one can be effective when executed in mosaic. The use of a third colour – the bluey-grey (as opposed to sticking with black) helps to give the urn a sense of place within the space. It is easy to imagine this piece being one of a set.

Indian Elephant

Designer and maker: Alison Slater
Medium: Cinca ceramic and gold leaf smalti
Size: 28 x 28 cm (11 x 11 in)
Date: 1997

I wanted to include this mosaic in contrast to the elephants on the tea trays (see page 66) to remind us of what an Indian Elephant looks like without his clothes on! The use of the subtly-speckled tiles which are the same colour as the rest of him, just to add a slight texture to the underbelly and feet, is inspired. Notice the circular *opus* on the elephant's back and how much it helps to reinforce the elephant's bulk and weight.

Klimt Box

Designer and maker: Jo Letchford
Medium: Vitreous glass and glass beads
Size: 40 x 10 x 30 cm (16 x 4 x 12 in)
Date: 1998

The rich, sumptuous materials found within the paintings of Gustav Klimt were the inspiration for this piece. The *opus regulatum* of certain areas is broken up by scrolls and waves in a whimsical and musical way. This would make a lovely sewing or quilting box.

Clown Fish Plaque

Designer: Martin Cheek   Maker: Laura Elson

There is a wonderful quality of depth to this mosaic. For the design to be seen to best effect in the finished work, it is important that the order of mosaicing is "nearest first" in a spatial sense. For example, the section of the fish's tail in front of the two strands of reed is mosaiced before the reed, which in turn is mosaiced in receding order as indicated by the codes R1 to R7 on the template on page 91. To add to the three-dimensional illusion, the reeds continue through the horizontal border at the base of the mosaic and over the side of the board.

You will need

16 black, 40 deep olive, 21 olive, 22 green, 34 lime green, 120 dark viridian, 67 light viridian, 164 flammè vert, 32 red, 60 orange, 40 tangerine and 2 white vitreous glass tiles

2 sheets of A4 carbon paper
Tracing paper
Sharp pencil
Crayons or coloured pencils
Sheets of newspaper
MDF, 15 mm (½ in) thick, approx. 30 x 30 cm (12 x 12 in)
Vitreous glass tiles, as shown above
Safety spectacles
Face mask
Mosaic nippers
125 ml (4 fl oz) wood adhesive in a dispenser
Tweezers or a cocktail stick
Rubber gloves
450 g (1 lb) powdered grout
Bowl of water
Mixing board for the grout
Stick to mix the grout
Plastic grout spreader
Cleaning cloth
Liquid floor cleaner
Abrasive cleaning pad
Pair of D rings with screws to hang your finished mosaic

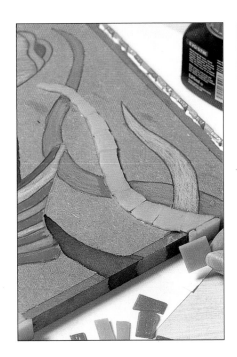

1 Enlarge the template on page 91 on a photocopier to the correct size, then transfer the design to the MDF board using carbon paper. Colour in the design. Mosaic the chequered vertical sides first using dark and light viridian half-tiles. Remember to incorporate the reeds in the bottom side as you work along it.

2 Mosaic the nearest reed first. The one that is visually behind it can now be added.

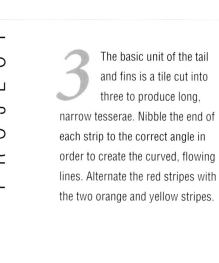

3 The basic unit of the tail and fins is a tile cut into three to produce long, narrow tesserae. Nibble the end of each strip to the correct angle in order to create the curved, flowing lines. Alternate the red stripes with the two orange and yellow stripes.

4 Now mosaic the remaining reeds, before starting on the eye and mouth. Tweezers or a cocktail stick can help with the fine positioning of the small pieces for the mouth, as shown in the detail. Note the triangular highlight in the eye.

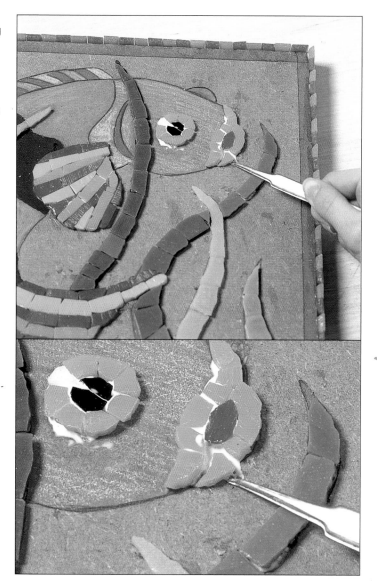

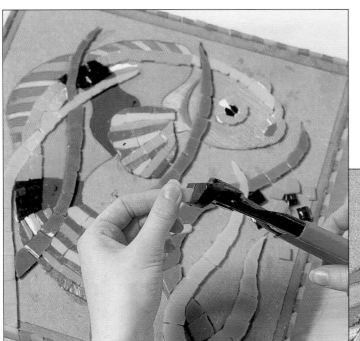

5 The pectoral fin is made in a similar way to the tail, using long narrow strips. Mosaic the strong key line along the fish's back and head. Note that the black markings are mosaiced as you go along and are not treated separately.

6 Flesh out the body and head following the curve of the key line. Although the direction of the *opus* follows the key line, remember to change colours at the appropriate points. "Crash through" the eye and reeds when you come to them. The illusion of three-dimensionality is enhanced if these lines appear to carry on through the reeds.

7 Add the dorsal fin. Once again, change colours at the appropriate points as you work. The fish is now complete.

8 Work on the border using quarter-tile dark viridian tesserae. Work around the reeds. Put in the *opus vermiculatum*. This is indicated by the broken lines on the template.

9 Complete the mosaic by filling in the background, following the flow of the *opus vermiculatum*. This is known as *opus musivum*.

10 Grout in the normal way. I wanted to show the grouting on this piece because it is always exciting when the grout is drawn across so many bright colours.

11 Wipe off the surface grout with a cloth, working in small circular movements. Rinse the cloth and change the water when necessary. The next day, clean off the residue scum with liquid floor cleaner and an abrasive cleaning pad. Screw the D rings to the back to hang the picture.

Indian Elephant Tea Tray

Designer: Martin Cheek   Maker: Jo Letchford

This nest of trays seems to suggest a family of father, mother and baby. I love the highly decorated elephants of India. The designs for the two largest trays were created by simply printing two of the wooden blocks that I had brought back from there, then enlarging them on the photocopier. I decided not to correct the obvious "mistake" showing the tusk emerging from the largest elephant's side, in favour of artistic authenticity. This design is worked indirect.

You will need

69 grey, 185 white, 1 black, 14 lime green, 51 dark green and 7 pink vein vitreous glass tiles
120 brown (or dark brown) ceramic mosaic tiles
82 gold leaf smalti tiles

Nest of trays, ready for painting (see Suppliers)
2 sheets of A4 carbon paper
Tracing paper
Sharp pencil
Crayons or coloured pencils
Sheets of newspaper
Waxed MDF board with kraft paper stretched on it (see p. 13)
Wallpaper paste
Soft paintbrush (Chinese paintbrushes are ideal)
Wooden skewer, tweezers or cocktail stick
450 g (1 lb) ready-mixed or powdered tile adhesive
Plastic mixing bowl or basin
Spoon to mix adhesive
3 mm notched trowel
Craft knife
Builder's float or a large flat piece of wood
Putty knife
Rubber gloves
450 g (1 lb) powdered grout
Bowl of water
Mixing board for the grout
Stick to mix the grout
Plastic grout spreader
Cleaning cloth
Liquid floor cleaner
Abrasive cleaning pad

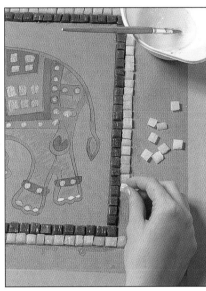

1 Enlarge the template on page 90 on a photocopier to the correct size for your tray and transfer the design to the stretched paper, using carbon paper. Colour in the design. This will act as a reminder as you work on the mosaicing.

2 Begin by mosaicing the border. Mix the wallpaper paste to quite a stiff consistency and paint a small area of the kraft paper at a time. As the tray design is worked indirect, the vitreous tesserae have to be placed flat-side down. Try to get the lines as straight as you can, not just on the outer edge, but on the inside too, so that you have a neat edge to work to when you come to the inner border.

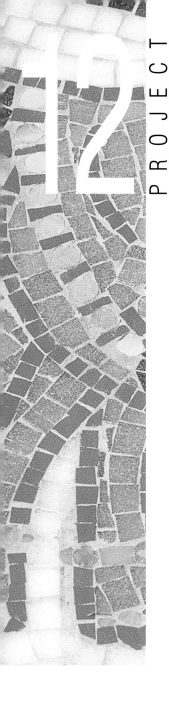

3 Mosaic the key line along the elephant's back from trunk to tail. For this I suggest using dark brown ceramic tesserae. The non-reflective ceramic contrasting with the shiny vitreous tesserae will reinforce the block-printed effect that I was trying to achieve with this design. The ceramic tesserae are flat on both sides, so there is no right or wrong way of laying them.

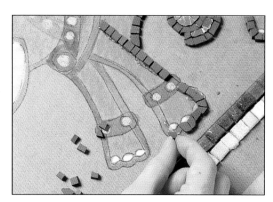

4 Continue mosaicing the brown ceramic tesserae until you have completed the entire outline of the elephant. Attention to detail in areas such as around the feet will pay off in the finished result. Allow the paste to set.

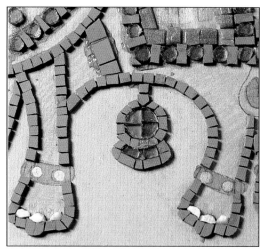

5 Add the white toes to the feet. Work in the gold leaf smalti alternately with the ceramic tesserae as you add the inner ceramic lines to the elephant's costume. You will find it easier if you pre-cut the small gold circles in batches. Make sure that the gold leaf smalti are gold-side down.

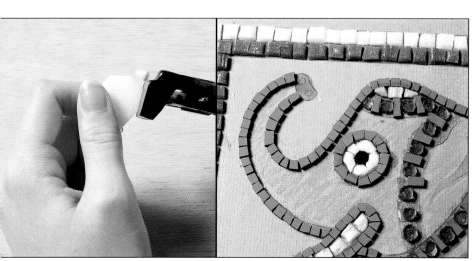

6 The iris of the elephant's eye is mainly made up of one tile trimmed to a circle, as shown in the close-up detail, then cut into four quarters. The middle of each quarter segment is then nibbled out and the tesserae placed back together to form their original circle. This is usually sufficient, but in this case we wanted a bigger eye, so we spread the quarters apart slightly and added a fifth one. The black pupil is added to fill the hole in the middle. Complete with a ring of brown tesserae.

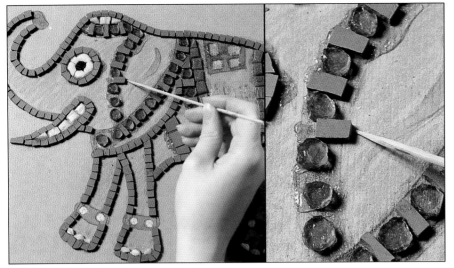

7 You can use a wooden skewer to help with fine positioning of the smaller tesserae.
I prefer tweezers. If you don't have either to hand then a cocktail stick will suffice.

8 My design showed the gold circles surrounded by green "material", but this proved to be too fussy. The compromise was to mosaic the anklets in one line, as shown here.

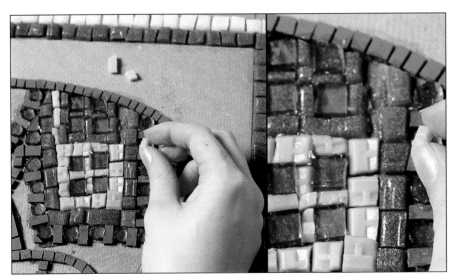

9 Mosaic the blanket next. Cut some quarter-tile tesserae in half to make two small rectangles, in order to achieve the necessary detail.

10 The elephant's nostrils were achieved in the same way as the eye, described in step 6. Mosaic the nearest one first, as it is the most important, then work the second one alongside it.

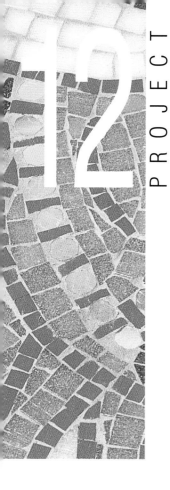

11 You are now ready to mosaic the elephant's grey skin. Divide each area up into key lines. You can see how, for example, on her head the key lines are along the trunk and around the eye. The line around the eye takes precedence over the one around the tusk and the hat. Once all four of these lines have been mosaiced, work outwards from them until the entire head is completed.

12 Mosaic all of the elephant's body, then start on the background. Begin by mosaicing the *opus vermiculatum* around the elephant.

13 In order to calm down this rich design, we decided to mosaic the background in *opus regulatum*, i.e. straight lines. Draw some horizontal lines across the design. As well as reminding you which direction to work in, this will also provide you with a guide to keep the horizontal lines from sloping up or down. When you have finished "papering" the mosaic, leave the paste to set.

14 Now it is time to stick the mosaic to the MDF tray. You will need to follow the specific mixing instructions for your tile adhesive, as these vary depending on the make. Once the adhesive is thoroughly mixed, comb it onto the tray using a notched trowel. Various depths of "notch" are available – we used a 3 mm one. Comb the adhesive in one direction only to avoid trapping any air.

15 Cut around your mosaic with a craft knife and slide it off the MDF board onto a flat surface. (New paper can be stretched on the board as described on page 13, so it can be used again and again.) With the help of a friend, flip the mosaic over and position it onto your tray. Try not to panic! So long as your wallpaper paste was mixed to a stiff enough consistency, the mosaic will hold.

If it doesn't hold and some tesserae drop off, restick them with paste, allow to dry, then try again. Once in position, push down the mosaic using a builder's float or a large piece of wood. Scrape off any excess adhesive which squeezes out from the edge, using a putty knife. Allow to set overnight – even if the instructions say that the adhesive sets in a few hours, I still advise you to be patient and wait until the following day.

16 This is the most exciting part. Using a cloth, soak the kraft paper with water and allow it to become thoroughly wet. Carefully and slowly remove the kraft paper. I find it helps if you pull the paper back on itself horizontally, rather than vertically. I like to try to remove the paper in one piece and keep it as a souvenir. If any tesserae come loose, stick them back into place with tile adhesive. Allow the tile adhesive to set.

Alternative design:
The Three Bears

Designer: Martin Cheek
Makers: Kerry Balman, Laura Elson and Naomi Hope

This continues the "family" theme suggested by the nest of trays. The opportunity to show the three bears holding out their porridge bowls in this cheerful and colourful design was too good to miss.

17 You can now grout your mosaic in the usual way using a grout spreader.

18 Clean off the surface grout with a damp cloth. Keep wringing out the cloth, and change the water frequently. Work the cloth in small circular movements to ensure that all the excess grout is removed.

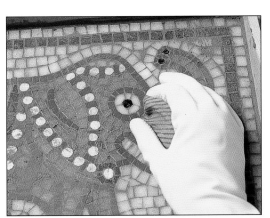

making mosaics/project 12

13 PROJECT A Fruit Table Top

Designer: Martin Cheek   Maker: Laura Elson

T his is a good example of "less is more". Limiting the elements of this pattern to incorporate only oranges and lemons does, I feel, make for a more coherent design. A circular table is likely to be used in the middle of a room and therefore the fact that the design works from all angles is a great bonus. The design is worked indirect.

You will need

9 black, 15 light grey, 16 white, 288 in shades of caramel, 57 in shades of dark orange, 33 tangerine, 37 lemon yellow and 20 bright yellow vitreous glass tiles

Wine table ready for painting
(see Suppliers)
Sheets of newspaper
Waxed MDF board with kraft paper stretched on it (see p. 13)
Long ruler
Sharp pencil
Protractor
6 sheets of A4 carbon paper
Wallpaper paste
Vitreous glass tiles, as shown above
Safety spectacles
Face mask
Mosaic nippers
Wooden skewer, tweezers or a cocktail stick
450 g (1 lb) ready mixed or powdered tile adhesive
Plastic mixing bowl or basin
Spoon to mix the adhesive
3 mm notched trowel
Putty knife
Craft knife
Cleaning cloth
Rubber gloves
450 g (1 lb) powdered grout
Metal tool to spread adhesive
Bowl of water
Mixing board for the grout
Stick for mixing the grout
Plastic grout spreader
Liquid floor cleaner
Abrasive cleaning pad

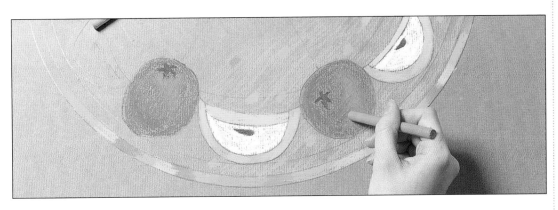

1 The mosaic for our table top had to measure 44 cm (17 ¼ in) in diameter to fit the table top snugly. A 5 mm (¼ in) gap all around was allowed to avoid any scratching caused by contact with the sharp mosaic edging. The easiest way to achieve the circle is to invert the table onto the paper and draw around it. You then need to establish the centre. To do this, hold one end of a long ruler so that it touches one side of the circle and swing it in an arc until you find the widest point. Draw a line connecting these two points and mark

the middle. Place a protractor on one side of the diameter with its centre on the centre of your circle. Mark off the points at 60 degrees and 120 degrees and do the same on the other side of the diameter. Draw lines through these marks and the centre point to divide your circle into six equal segments. Using the template on page 90, enlarged on a photocopier to fit, draw a circle of six oranges and six lemon slices – a slice of lemon in the middle of each segment and an orange on each segment line.

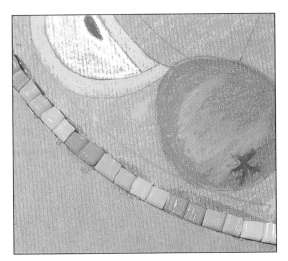

2 Colour in the design. Work indirect throughout, applying wallpaper paste as you go along and placing the flat side of the tesserae downwards. Mosaic the border using orange, tangerine and lemon tesserae. As well as keeping to a neat outer line, try to create a neat inner line, too.

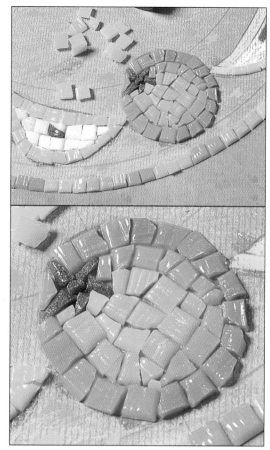

3 Mosaic a lemon slice. Begin by making the outer yellow rind. Although a real lemon would have a soft colour along the top, I have made it the same strong yellow so that it doesn't visually "dissolve" into the beige background. (It is interesting that only when this fact has been pointed out to you, you begin to question the "realism" of these lemon slices.) Fill in the centre of the lemon slice by making two neat rows of white tesserae. Once again I have exaggerated the colour of the pips to brown so that they stand out sufficiently. Mosaic the stalk of an orange.

4 Mosaic an orange around the stalk. Getting the outer line neat is the most important thing. Work in concentric circles to fill in the centre.

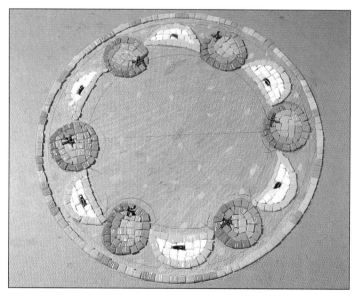

5 Continue working around the design until you have mosaiced all six oranges and lemon wedges.

6 Mosaic the *opus vermiculatum*. Because the oranges and lemons touch, this *opus* is divided in two and runs along the inside and outside of the circle of fruit.

7 Fill in the "dips" between the oranges with beige tesserae, adding the odd orange one to keep the colour lively. Try to establish a circular movement. Continue to work inwards for one more row.

8 The best way to ensure neat concentric circles from this point on is to draw them onto the paper. Place various sized cups, saucers and plates onto the centre of your design and draw around them. Mosaic a circle that is a convenient distance away from the *opus vermiculatum*. You can now work outwards from this line to fill in the gap.

9 Now work inwards from the circular line towards the centre. It is a good idea to place one circular tesserae in the middle to "aim" for, as shown here. Allow the wallpaper paste to set overnight.

making mosaics/project 13

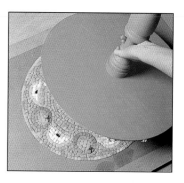

10 It is time to stick the mosaic to the MDF table. Follow the specific mixing instructions for your tile adhesive, as these vary depending on the make. Once the adhesive is thoroughly mixed, comb it onto the table using a notched trowel. Various depths of "notch" are available – we used a 3 mm one, which corresponds to the thickness of the vitreous glass tiles. Comb the adhesive in circular movements to cover the table top.

11 Having completely covered the table top with the adhesive, comb over it again in one direction only to avoid trapping any air in the adhesive.

12 Pick up the table and slowly lower it down onto the mosaic. It helps if you have a friend to line up the table with the mosaic. Take your time and try not to panic. When you are sure that the table and mosaic are correctly lined up, with even spaces all round, press the table firmly into place. Scrape off any excess adhesive which squeezes out from the edge using a putty knife. Allow to set overnight – even if the instructions say that the adhesive sets in a few hours.

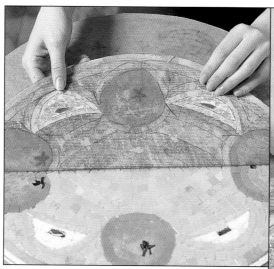

13 The moment of truth! Cut the papered mosaic away from the waxed board with a craft knife. Using a cloth, soak the paper with water and allow it to become thoroughly wet. Carefully and slowly remove the kraft paper, pulling it horizontally rather than vertically. Finally, grout the mosaic in the usual way.

Alternative Designs:
Bananas & Pears Table

Designer and maker: Emma Abel

The strong choice of colours gives this table a 1950's look. Once again the palette is limited. Emma has used thick floor tiles for her table, so when the mosaic was set in place, we used a trowel with deeper notches in order to have a deeper bed of adhesive.

Fruity Table

Designers: Martin Cheek and Andrew Higgins

Makers: Martin Cheek and Danny Branscombe Kent

This was our original design for a fruit table. We changed the rectangular arrangement of fruit to a circular one and simplified it to make the design for the main project.

Thyme Paving
Slab

Designer and maker: Danny Branscombe Kent

Those design cleverly incorporates the "negative space" created by the interstices – the gaps between the tesserae – to describe the stalks of the thyme. This is one of the more complex projects as it relies heavily on getting the background "grid" straight, both horizontally and vertically. The lines of the grid must continue on visually "behind" the thyme for the illusion to work. This project requires precision work and lots of patience if you want to get a result as accurate as Danny's, but I'm sure you'll agree that it's worth the effort! This piece is worked indirect and is suitable for setting in the ground outdoors.

You will need

12 in shades of white, 27 dark grey and 20 green vitreous glass tiles

20 dark brown and 67 speckled brown ceramic mosaic tiles

Sheet of A4 carbon paper
Sharp pencil
Sheets of newspaper
Waxed MDF board with kraft paper stretched on it
Crayons or coloured pencils
Cinca and vitreous glass tiles
Safety spectacles
Face mask
Mosaic nippers
Wallpaper paste
Wooden skewer, tweezers or a cocktail stick
4 lengths of 2 x 1 timber approx. 25-30 cm (9¾-12 in) long
Soft paint brush (Chinese paint brushes are ideal)
Petroleum Jelly
PVA wood adhesive
Tea strainer
Rubber gloves
450 g (1 lb) powdered grout
Piece of chicken wire
Wire cutters
450 g (1 lb) quick drying cement
Plastic mixing bowl or basin
Small builder's trowel
Hammer
Craft knife
Toothbrush
Cleaning cloth
Bowl of water
Mixing board for the grout
Stick to mix the grout
Plastic grout spreader
Liquid floor cleaner
Abrasive cleaning pad
Wood stain/black powder paint
15 mm (½ in) paint brush

1 Enlarge the template on page 93 on a photocopier to approximately 21 cm (8¼ in) square, then transfer the design to the stretched paper using carbon paper. Colour in the design clearly in strong colours, as this clean graphic quality will help you to focus on the mosaic detail. The size of the slab has been dictated by the fact that the background is divisible by exactly seven squares plus a sufficient gap for the grid lines. Allow a half-tile width all round for the border. Draw in the grid lines 3 mm (⅛ in) wide. This is as thick as the grout will be on the finished slab.

2 Work indirect throughout. You can see from this picture how tightly Danny is working and how rigidly she is sticking to her drawing. Remember to place the glass tesserae flat-side down. Cutting those inner curves takes a lot of practice, and you will invariably get lots of wastage – persevere and be patient! Using the "wrong" side of the nippers can help.

3 The thyme leaves are made by cutting across the tiles diagonally in order to get them as large as possible. Once again you will need to be patient and be prepared to make lots of attempts at getting the leaves into neat tear-drop shapes. Use a skewer, tweezers or a cocktail stick for fine positioning.

4 Next, paste down the quarter-tile tesserae that make up the border. Where the thyme crosses over the border you will need to nibble lines out to allow for the stalks.

5 Mosaic the background, nibbling out the thyme stalks as you go. In this detail, the background tile third up on the left and also the bottom tile on the right have been cut into two and then had a "V" nibbled out of them for the petals before being reassembled. If you look carefully, you can just make out the hairline crack.

6 Drawing the stalk on the tile itself can help you to cut it accurately. Don't get too preoccupied with trying to get all of the elements out of one tile. Getting the angles right is a more important consideration and it may well take a number of tiles to achieve this. Continue until you have finished "papering" the whole mosaic, then leave overnight for the paste to dry.

7 You are now ready to make the mould which will contain the concrete. Arrange the four lengths of timber batons around the mosaic. Paint petroleum jelly, which will act as a release agent, on the inside surface of the batons, where they will come in contact with the concrete.

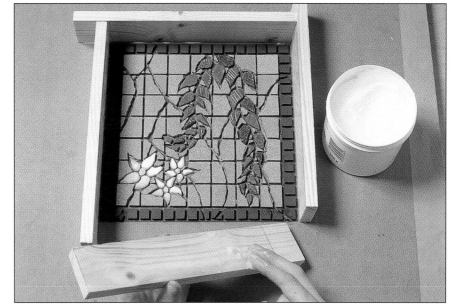

8 Using PVA wood adhesive, glue the batons to the paper about 5 mm (¼ in) away from the border. To prevent any possibility of leakage, I usually run a bead of glue all around the outside of the batons and up the outer edge where they join. The paper on the waxed board offers a temporary surface to glue the batons to. They can be hammered off later. Allow the glue to set.

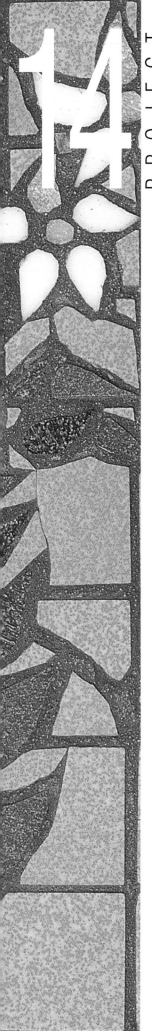

9 Using a tea strainer, sprinkle a small amount of powdered grout onto the top surface of the mosaic and carefully brush it into the interstices. The grout acts as a barrier and prevents the concrete from flowing under the tesserae and onto the surface of the mosaic. Make sure there is no grout left on the top surface of the mosaic as this will prevent the cement from "keying".

10 Cut a piece of chicken wire to the same size as the slab. Place it in the mould to make sure it fits snugly. Any extra wire can be bent over and squashed down flat. When you are satisfied, remove the wire from the mould. Mix up the quick-drying cement according to the instructions on the packet and pour it into the mould. Use a small builder's trowel to spread the cement smoothly and evenly. This type of cement is not as hard as ordinary sand and cement, but for a slab of this size it is fine. When I make slabs larger than 30 cm (12 in) square, I use sand and cement.

11 Push the chicken wire into the cement, so that it lies beneath the surface. The chicken wire strengthens the cement and acts as insurance – if you accidentally drop the slab, the chicken wire should hold it while you glue it back together with more quick-drying cement. On slabs larger than 30 cm (12 in) square, I recommend that you also insert metal reinforcement rods available from builder's merchants. Top up the mould with the remaining cement.

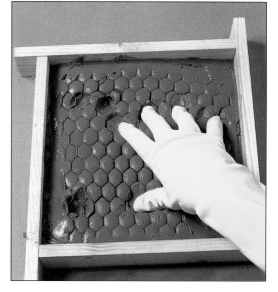

12 Leave to harden. The brand that I use sets in a couple of hours but the time varies depending on the room temperature and the amount of water that you add to the mix. Remove the wooden batons by gently tapping them away with a hammer. They are only glued to the brown kraft paper and will come away quite easily. Cut the papered mosaic away from the waxed board using a craft knife.

13 Turn the slab over and remove the paper by first soaking it with water. If the board has been properly waxed, the paper should peel away very easily. Brush away any excess grout that is still in the interstices, using a toothbrush. Grout in the normal way. Allow to dry for a day before cleaning off the surface scum with floor cleaner using an abrasive pad.

14 We decided that the grout needed to be stained a darker colour with wood stain in order to pick out the thyme leaves. Another way of achieving a darker grout is to add black powder paint to it at the dry powder stage.

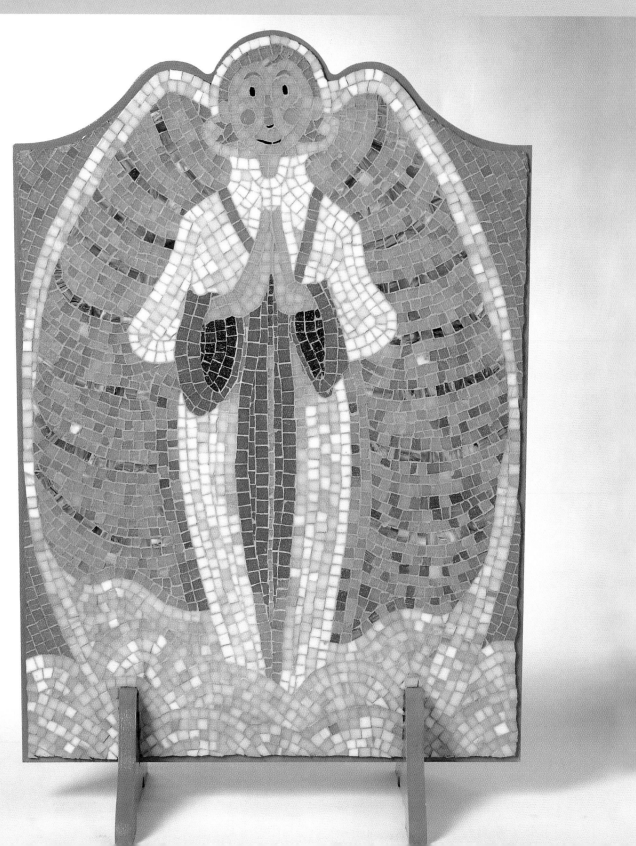

A firescreen is a practical and decorative piece for a room in summer when the fireplace is not in use. It can offer a serene focus, like the angel shown here. Andrew Higgins' delicate design captures the essence of individual personality with the minimum of lines. The idea for this angel was suggested by the shape of the firescreen itself – those gothic curves seemed to be crying out to be used as wings. If we imagine the curve in the middle of the screen to be his head, then the angel appears automatically, as if by magic.

You will need

67 dark blue (cuffs and cassock), 9 grey, 3 dark pink (not shown), 69 background blue, 60 gold-veined dark blue, 3 black, 19 dark grey, 281 in shades of pale blue, 45 in shades of light pink, 432 white vitreous glass tiles

6 sheets of A4 carbon paper
Tracing paper
Sharp pencil
Sheets of newspaper
MDF firescreen blank (see Suppliers)
Crayons or coloured pencils
Vitreous glass tiles as shown above
Safety spectacles
Face mask
Mosaic nippers
125 ml (4 fl oz) wood adhesive in a dispenser
Rubber gloves
450 g (1 lb) powdered grout
Bowl of water
Mixing board for the grout
Lollipop stick
Plastic grout spreader
Cleaning cloth
Liquid floor cleaner
Abrasive cleaning pad

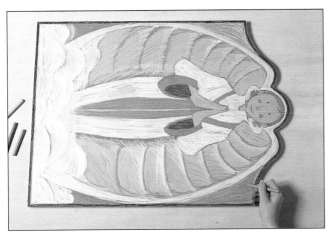

1 Enlarge the template on page 92 on a photocopier to the size of your MDF blank. Transfer the design to your firescreen blank using carbon paper and colour in the design.

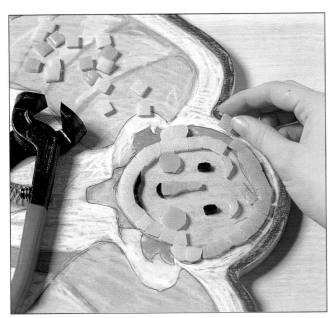

2 We started on the face. Mosaic the key line in light pink round the face. Add the features. It's worth playing with these until you are satisfied. For example, you may wish to make a number of eyes and choose the pair that give the desired expression. It's amazing what a difference a tiny change can make to the overall expression – I find myself agonizing for hours over this! Add the key line of the hair before finishing off the forehead.

3 Mosaic a circle of flesh-coloured tesserae around the eyes. It helps to let the eyes set before doing this, so that you don't disturb them and spoil the expression. Finish off the face and add the ruff. Notice that you add the ruff before the neck because it is the nearer, visually speaking, and "contains" the neck.

4 Mosaic the cuffs in dark blue. In the case of the sleeves, try to feel the way in which the fabric is falling. Think of the folds created by the arm inside the sleeve. The line of dark grey tesserae can then be carefully mosaiced to describe this, as shown in the detail. It really helps to break every shape up into key lines. Always mosaic the nearest thing first, in this case the key line of the cuffs before the hands, then the vertical lines that make up the edge of the cassock. For the hands, work the main outer line first, then the inner line, and finally the spaces in between.

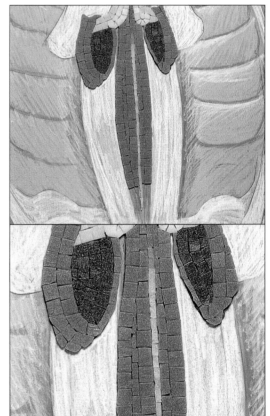

5 The same rule applies to the clouds. It is necessary to mosaic the key lines, working from the bottom up, before you can finish the two vertical outer white lines of the cassock.

6 Every shape can be divided up in many different ways. My rule is always to "let the *opus* describe the form". You can see how dividing the neck area up into curved lines, echoing the shoulders, is the best solution. Draw the lines on as a guide to the positioning of the tesserae.

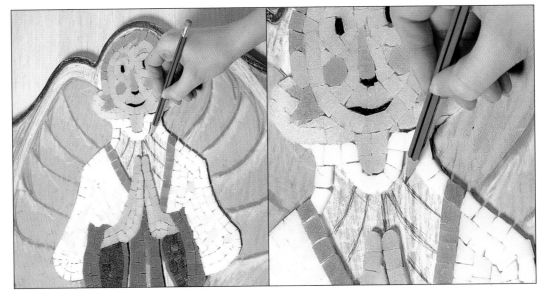

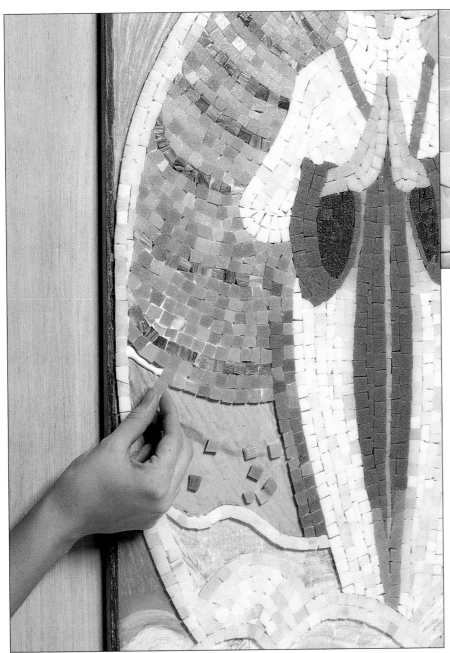

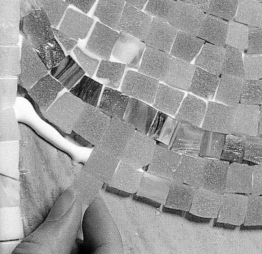

7 Gradually work your way down the wings incorporating the lines of darker blue-and-gold veined tesserae as you go. The exact positioning of these lines is not important, just add them at a convenient point. Use a mixture of pale blue tiles to create the iridescence of the wings.

8 This close-up picture shows one of the dark blue lines being added.

9 Filling in the clouds is achieved by working from the key line downward, "crashing" into the clouds on either side and below.

artist's tip

The splinters that fall as waste can be recycled to make the small details in the angel's mouth and nose. If these small triangular pieces keep falling over, it isn't your fault – they come from the bevelled edge of the tile. They needn't be discarded, though – simply use another tessera to prop them up while the glue sets.

10 When you come to the place where the foot of the firescreen goes, glue the foot in position and wait for the glue to set. Once it is set, you can mosaic right up to the foot without the risk of moving it.

11 When you have finished mosaicing the entire screen, allow it to set, then grout it in the normal way. You have to be brave – even for me, after all these years, slopping that grey muddy porridge onto a beautiful mosaic always feels like an act of wanton destruction. Five minutes later, however, when it has been worked into the interstices and the lines of flow are delineated by the grout, everything feels right with the world once more.

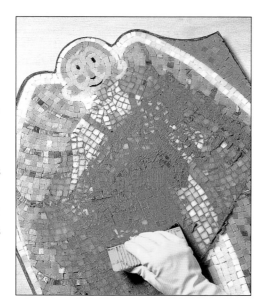

12 I wanted to show the grouting on this project because the grey grout is at its most pronounced when applied to pure white mosaic.

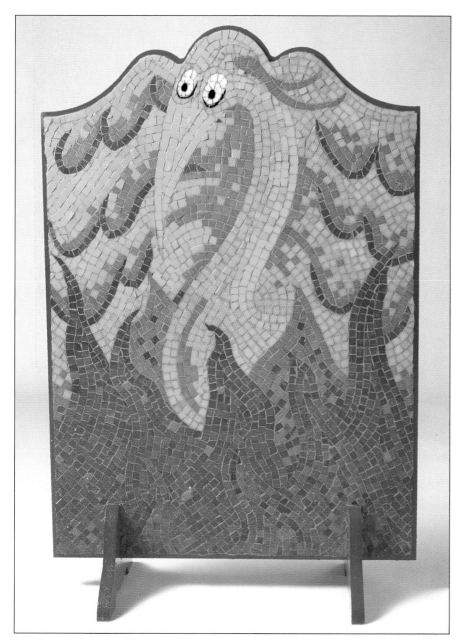

Alternative design:

Fiery Phoenix

Designer: Martin Cheek

Makers: Martin Cheek and Danny Branscombe Kent

I designed this fiery phoenix arising from the sizzling flames as a contrast to all that calm serenity radiating from the angel. Obviously you could, if you wished, mosaic the two designs on either side of the same firescreen and choose which one you wanted to present to the room, depending on your mood!

Templates

Indian Elephant
Tea Tray
(page 66)

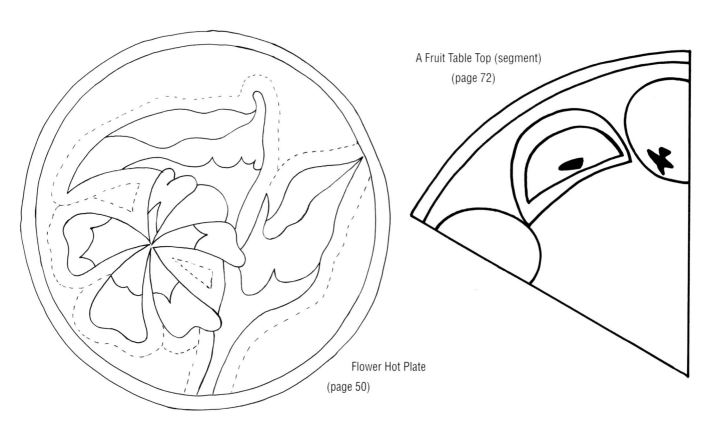

A Fruit Table Top (segment)
(page 72)

Flower Hot Plate
(page 50)

Guinea Fowl Plaque
(page 54)

R7

R6

R1

R4

R3

R6

R2

R5

R7

Clown Fish Plaque
(page 60)

making mosaics/templates

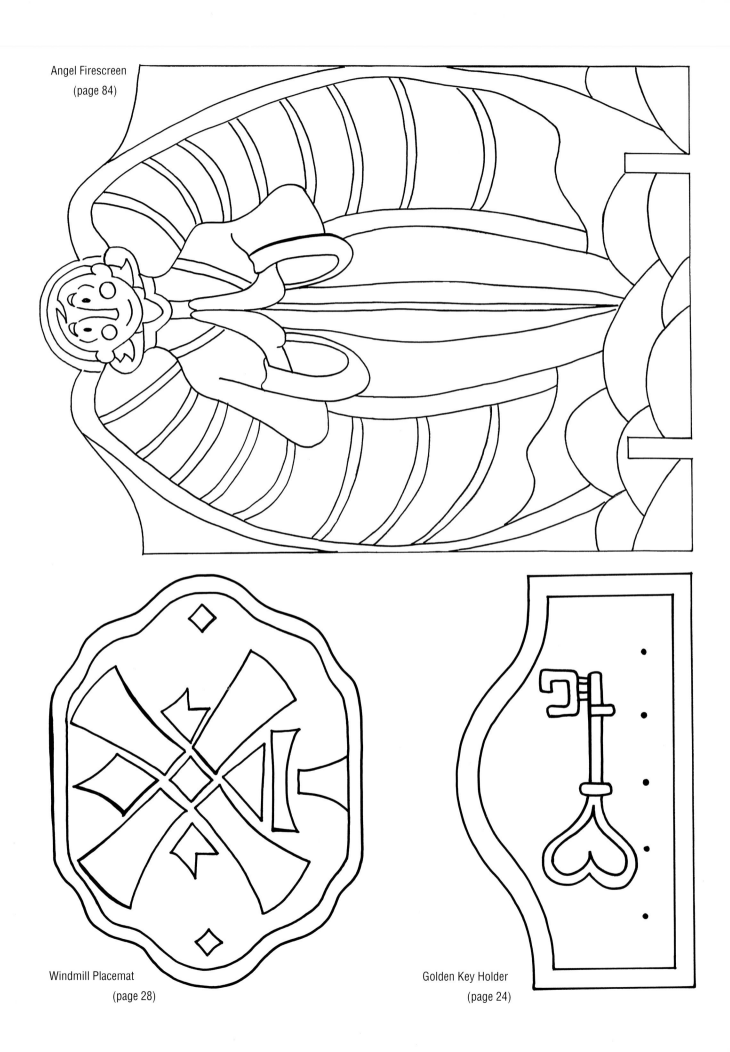

Angel Firescreen
(page 84)

Windmill Placemat

(page 28)

Golden Key Holder

(page 24)

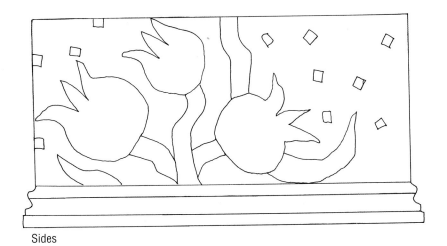

Jewellery Box
(page 46)

Sides

Lid

Endpieces

Thyme Paving Slab
(page 78)

Tree-of-life Cachepot
(page 34)

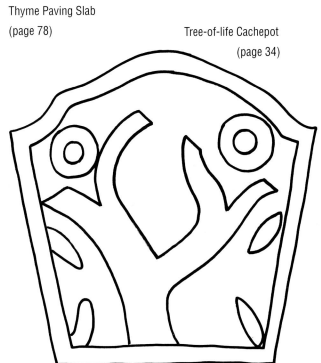

making mosaics/templates

Suppliers

UK

Martin Cheek Mosaic Kits:
Tile Packs for projects in this book and *Mosaics in a Weekend*. Each pack contains tiles in the quantities and colours required for the chosen project with an allowance for wastage. Suppliers of mixed bags of vitreous glass, gold mirror, gold leaf smalti, coloured smalti and glazed ceramic tesserae and a range of mosaic kits designed by Martin Cheek.
For details of products and prices, please send a stamped, addressed envelope to: Martin Cheek Mosaic Kits, 93 Stone Road, Broadstairs, Kent, CT10 1ET. Tel: 01843 867481 Fax: 01843 868912
http://www.mosaicart-cheek.demon.co.uk
e-mail: martin@mosaicart-cheek.demon.co.uk

D.W & G. Heath (Croyden) Ltd
19 Portley Wood Road, Whyteleafe
Surrey CR3 0BQ
Tel: 020 8657 6349 / 01883 344864
Large stockist of mosaic tools and materials
(Vitreous glass, smalti, glazed and unglazed ceramic tesserae)

Edgar Udny & Co. Ltd
314 Balham High Road
London SW17
Tel: 020 8767 8181
UK's largest stockist of mosaic tools and materials
(Vitreous glass, smalti, glazed and unglazed ceramic tesserae)

Reed Harris Ltd
Riverside House, 27 Carnworth Road
London SW6 3HR
Tel: 020 7736 7511
(Marble and ceramic tiles; unglazed Cinca tiles from Portugal; full range of Ardex materials)

Scumble Goosie (Contact: John Madeley)
Lewiston Mill, Brimscombe
Stroud, Gloustershire
Tel: 01453 731305
(MDF blanks: boxes, fire screen, wine table, etc.)

Homecrafts Direct
PO Box 38
Leicester LE1 9BU
Tel: 0116 2513139
Fax: 0116 2515015
e-mail: post@speccrafts.demon.co.uk

Paint Creative Products
Outlets throughout the UK; phone for your nearest store.
40 High Street, Royal Tunbridge Wells
Kent TN1 1XF
Tel: 01892 519990
Fax: 01892 618 910
http://www.paint-creative.com
(Paints, glazes, varnishes, stencils, furniture and accessories to decorate)

Romantique Mosaic Centre
12 Pulteney Bridge
Bath BA2 4AY
Tel: 01225 463 073

Panduro Hobby
Westway House, Transport Avenue
Brentford, Middx TW8 9HF
Tel: 020 8847 6161
Fax: 020 8847 5073

Antrad Ltd
Old Flour Mill, Queen Street
Emsworth, Hants PO10 7BT
Tel: 01243 388 600
Fax: 01243 388 605

SOUTH AFRICA

Nationwide suppliers of mosaic tiles, adhesives, grouting and cutting tools:

Just Tiles
To find the branch closest to you, call
0800 22 92 82 or your local number from the list below:

Cape Town Tel: (021) 510-5555
Johannesburg Tel: (011) 455-5500
Durban Tel: (031) 332-8581
Port Elizabeth Tel: (041) 413-602
Bloemfontein Tel: (051) 448-1309

Italtile
To find the branch closest to you, call your local number from the list below:

Cape Town Tel: (021) 448-2450
Bellville Tel: (021) 75-8442
Alberton Tel: (011) 902-4601
Randburg Tel: (011) 886-4760
Pretoria Tel: (012) 348-8700
Durban Tel: (031) 37-8344

CTM
To find the branch closest to you, call your local number from the list below:

Brackenfell Tel: (021) 981-4576
Montague Gardens Tel: (021) 552-2999
Tokai Tel: (021) 715-8506
Edenvale Tel: (011) 453-0320
Randburg Tel: (011) 792-4136
Roodepoort Tel: (011) 674-2134
Springs Tel: (011) 817-1336
Redhill Park, Durban Tel: (031) 579-4245
George Tel: (044) 871-1021
Bloemfontein Tel: (051) 430-4967

AUSTRALIA

Alan Patrick Pty Ltd
11 Agnes St
Jolimont, VIC 3002
Tel: (02) 9211 1586
Fax: (02) 9211 1587
(Vitreous glass tiles, smalti and other mosaic supplies)

Academy Tiles
20 Herbert St
Artarmon, NSW 2064
Tel: (02) 9436 3566

Ceramic and Craft Centre
52 Wecker Road
Mansfield, QLD 4122
Tel: (07) 3343 7377

Glass Craft Australia
54-56 Lexton Road
Box Hill North, VIC 3129
Tel: (03) 9897 4188
Fax: (03) 9897 4344
(Vitreous glass tiles, tools, books, adhesives, grout)

Lincraft
Gallery Level, Imperial Arcade
Pitt Street, Sydney, NSW 2000
Tel: (02) 9221 5111

Queen Street
Brisbane, QLD 4000
Tel: (07) 3221 0064

303 Lt Collins Street
Melbourne, VIC 3000
Tel: (03) 9650 1609

NEW ZEALAND

Handcraft Supplies Ltd
13-19 Rosebank Road
Avondale
Tel: (09) 8289834

NZ Hobby Clay & Craft Co Ltd
1/80 James Fletcher Drive
Mangere
Tel: (09) 270 0140

Spotlight
Head Office
Tel: (09) 262 5090

The Tile Company
782 Great South Road
Penrose
Tel: (09) 525 5793

Trendy Trims Ltd
7 Angle Street
Onehunga
Tel: (09) 634 4531

Acknowledgements

Glossary

I would like to take the opportunity to thank all of my friends and colleagues who have been so supportive, particularly:

Yvonne McFarlane, who commissioned this book and hasn't lost her patience or sense of humour with this ever-trying author.

Rosemary Wilkinson, who knew nothing about mosaic when we started this book but is now an expert. Thanks for your patience, intelligence and thoroughness.

Colin Bowling who not only took the photographs brilliantly but was always on the ball when the rest of us were "mosaiced up".

The Cheeky mosaic team which consists of:

My main assistant Danny Branscombe Kent and her bump, which has already overtaken mine and will be a bump no longer when this book comes out!
Assistant assistants: Laura Elson and Kerry Balman; Kerry was also our hand model.

The guest professional mosaic artists are:

Emma Abel, Abel Mosaics, 36 Westwell Road, London SW16 5RT. Tel: 020 8679 9591
email: emma_abel@hotmail.com

Jo Letchford, 25 Beverley Road, Canterbury, Kent, CT2 7EN. Tel: 01227 472476

Maria Starling, 62B Navarino Road, London E8 1AQ. Tel: 020 7275 7613 /020 8692 0009
mobile: 0777 551 7409

Collette Price, 66 Broadfield View, Kilcullen Road, Naas, Co. Kildare, Ireland. Tel: 00353 45 894239, mobile: 00353 87231 0043

All are available for commissioned work.

Another mosaic artist whose work appears in the gallery section:

Emma J.F.E. Ropner, Hill Top East, Newton-Le-Willows, Bedale, North Yorkshire, DL8 1TP.
Tel: 01677 424049 mobile: 07710 680607
email: emma@hilltopeast22.freeserve.co.uk

Grateful thanks also to:

Scumble Goosie for supplying all the blanks used in this book (see list of suppliers).

Paint Creative Products for supplying their beautiful range of water-based, soft sheen acrylics (see list of suppliers).

Alan Welcome, who continues to produce and market the Martin Cheek Mosaic Kits so brilliantly.

Andrew Higgins, whose opinion I find invaluable and who was kind enough to help with the design work.

Rex Hope for allowing us to use Sickert's studio.

MOSAIC COURSE INFORMATION

Martin Cheek runs three-day weekend mosaic courses at his and his wife's home in Broadstairs, Kent. For information about courses please write to: Flint House, 21 Harbour Street, Broadstairs, Kent, CT10 1ET, England, enclosing a large, stamped, addressed envelope.

Andamento The generic word to describe the general "flow" of the mosaic, e.g. the andamento of the Fruit Table Top on page 72 is circular.

Direct method The most basic and common technique for the laying of mosaic. Tesserae are cut and stuck, face up, directly onto the base. The surface of mosaics made using this technique are therefore not always smooth, and much licence can be taken with the shape and texture of tesserae.

Indirect method A mosaic-laying technique often used for large-scale work, usually intended for outdoor sittings. Tesserae are stuck face down on to paper with a temporary, water-based bonding agent (generally gum arabic or wallpaper paste). The mosaic can then be transported if necessary, whole or in sections, and set in its permanent base with the paper side uppermost. The paper is then peeled away to reveal the finished work. The resulting surface is therefore usually smooth, and best grouted.

Opus regulatum A Roman mosaic technique whereby regular, square tesserrae are applied in straight rows. The result is like a "brick wall" pattern and was frequently used to fill expanses of background.

Opus vermiculatum A Roman mosaic technique whereby regular, square tesserrae are applied in a row around the main mosaic motif to create a halo effect and emphasize the setting lines of the design. *Vermis* is the Latin word for worm, (e.g. vermicelli) so you can think of this as the "worm" of tesserae that outline the main figure(s) (see the Indian Elephant Tea Tray). If the *opus vermiculatum* is continued outwards to fill a larger area, then this area becomes *opus musivum* (see the Guinea Fowl Plaque and the Clown Fish Plaque)

Tesserae "Tessera" is a Roman word meaning cube. These cubes are the basic building blocks of mosaic. The term embraces diverse materials including marble, ceramic, glass, broken crockery, mirror glass, stones and pebbles.

Index